E. R. F Hart

The Heart of the West

An American Story

E. R. F Hart

The Heart of the West
An American Story

ISBN/EAN: 9783744665612

Printed in Europe, USA, Canada, Australia, Japan

Cover: Foto ©Thomas Meinert / pixelio.de

More available books at **www.hansebooks.com**

THE
Heart of the West:

An American Story.

By an Illinoian.

Time: 1860.   Scene: On the Mississippi.

"The mystic chords of memory, stretching from hundreds of battlefields, will yet swell the chorus of the Union, if touched, as surely they will be, by the better angels of our nature."—*Lincoln.*

"The Valley of the Mississippi is, upon the whole, the most magnificent dwelling-place prepared by God for man's abode."—*De Tocqueville.*

CHICAGO:
STEAM PRINTING HOUSE OF HAND & HART.
1871.

DEDICATION.

TO THE

RT. REV. HENRY B. WHIPPLE, D. D.,

OF MINNESOTA,

HON. MILLARD FILLMORE,

OF NEW YORK,

And those eminent men of Illinois, and her agents and creditors abroad, who aided in saving the State from ruin, by engrafting in her SECOND CONSTITUTION *a sound policy relating to her public debt,—this little volume is respectfully dedicated, with the hope that whatever its faults, it will not be found wholly unworthy of their notice, and that abler pens may be brought to the support of a noble cause.*

PREFACE.

THE press is in our day one of the great levers by which masses of opinion are to be moved, and the resulting action secured; and *romance* is now the acceptable dress in which truth must be arrayed and presented to the public.

And although error, too, chooses this vesture, yet the fact is undeniable, that in our day the world has received and acted upon much that is valuable through this means.

And there are certain simple and salutary truths that seem to be unrecognized in the practical working of the public mind; and certain evils, so enormous that to be named should be enough, seem also to be unrecognized. And trusting that it may contribute, in some degree, to the ultimate adjustment of this "Grand Balance," and to a public recognition of the errors, as well as the losses and gains, of the past few years, and to the healthy adjustment of affairs on a sound basis,—this little book is respectfully submitted to the public, with the hope that its faults may be overlooked, and that abler writers may be induced to labor in this field.

Events that have occurred in Europe within the last ten days have shown what a miserable failure is so-called statesmanship; how readily the appeal is made to force; how slight the power of civilization and refinement to prevent a resort to violence, and how terribly the human race are afflicted by a want of the application of the principles of Christianity, and common-sense, to statesmanship, and how exceedingly rare, on this earth, is combined wisdom, power and magnanimity.

The story of Grey Eagle was suggested, and in part founded upon actual facts, that came under the personal knowledge of the author, in the far West years ago,—circumstances of vile outrage and wrong against the Indians, so flagrant and dastardly that they never can be forgotten.

In the conversation upon political subjects, historical facts are given that are believed to be the key to much that is false and wrong,—much hypocrisy, corruption and violence,—and the conclusions to which the argument of the book points are believed to be in harmony with the recorded opinions of the great men who, under God, laid the foundations of our Government; in perfect accord with Christianity, applied to statesmanship, with the most practical common-sense, the best experience, and the plainest truth.

Partisanship and Sectionalism are now with us the monsters that stand in the way of truth, and, for a time at least, the walls and thorny hedges that divide parties should be cleared away, and the great field of truth laid open for full and just examination. Old errors should be fully understood and admitted, in order that present errors may be abated; and this should be done in a spirit of lofty candor, and a sacred regard for TRUTH in every point of political history. Starting with the known and incontrovertible facts, the unknown deeps of error may be sounded if not explored, and their secrets revealed, and the superficial bombast of mere partisan literature give place to the clear light of that accurate and faithful history which alone is valuable as a guide; that lamp of experience that may guide our feet, and whose light is always truly reflected and increased by Revelation.

GRAND PRAIRIE, ILL.,
July 21st, 1870.

CHAPTER I.

ON a calm and beautiful spring morning, late in the month of April, A. D. 1860, a large raft of pine lumber, from the St. Croix Pineries, may have been seen entering the head of Lake Pepin, on the Upper Mississippi. The lake is but a widening of the river, and its deep, still waters furnish but little current to hasten the raftsman on his way; and, as its length is about thirty miles, the passage is necessarily slow and tedious.

At the time of which we write, the vast forests upon the upper waters of the Great River had been pierced in every direction by the hardy lumbermen, and the sound of the ax and saw, the buzz of machinery, and the bustle of towns and trade, had become far more common than the wilder sounds that broke the solitude of an earlier period. Great quantities of lumber were annually manufactured, and rafted from points *above* the *pineless region* to the river towns in Minnesota and Wisconsin, and lower down the river, to the various landing places, towns and cities, of Iowa, Illinois and Missouri, while occasionally a raft would descend the river to the "Lower Country," that is, to the Mississippi River front of Arkansas and Kentucky, Tennessee, Mississippi and Louisiana. The raft to which we have referred, one of the largest size, and made up of lumber selected carefully for that especial market, was destined for the "Coast," that is, the beautiful delta of *then* highly cultivated lands that fringed the banks of the river, for some distance above

New Orleans, and that might then claim to be the garden of America.

The tent-like cabins built upon the clean and odorous boards, "joist," "scantling," &c., of which this floating island of lumber was composed, were constructed of new and perfectly clean boards, were arranged with order and neatness, and an air of quiet comfort pervaded the group of men a little "aft" the centre of the raft, who were looking intently upon some object far down the lake.

"It is a steamboat," cried one of the raftsmen who had taken his stand upon a coop on the forward part of the raft.

"The first boat of the season," said several at once.

"Her swell will help widen the channel of open water for us through yonder ice," said one, who appeared to be the owner or master of the raft; "although this mild weather would soon finish it," he quickly added; "and now, boys, for breakfast."

The last speaker was a young man of perhaps twenty-seven years of age, about five feet eleven inches in height, of a manly form, but not athletic, blue eyes, and rather pale face, with a grave and earnest expression, like that of a man who had known but few holidays in life.

Walter Sydenham was born on the Atlantic coast, the cold and rocky northeast, and reared in Wisconsin, where he was left an orphan, at a tender age, to struggle with bitter poverty. Inheriting a love of books from his mother, he had made them his solace and companions. Somewhat impulsive and imaginative, he was yet practical and reflective, with his own ideas of duty, honor and religion. In temperament, the sanguine and nervous might be said to predominate, with very little of the bilious.

Coming to the new territory of Minnesota at the age

of twenty, and working as a hired laborer, he had, by industry and attention to business, accumulated some property, and was now engaged in the business of lumbering. Sprung from English ancestry, he possessed the English qualities of firmness, straight-forwardness and a love of "fair play."

At the call of Sydenham, the raftsmen, ten in number, gathered near the largest cabin, which stood rather towards the left, or "larboard" side of the raft, about forty feet back of the center, and directly opposite one on the right of the center. There was a third cabin some seventy-five feet forward of these, which was the sitting and sleeping room of Sydenham and his guests.

After performing their morning ablutions, the whole party sat down to a substantial breakfast of fish from the lake, fried; broiled venison, boiled potatoes, fried cakes, honey, bread, butter, coffee, &c. As the raft was provided with a good cooking-stove, a pretty good cook, (an intelligent lad of sixteen) and was well supplied with stores, the preparation of a comfortable meal was at all times practicable, and cleanliness, order, regularity and good cooking were the rule.

The meal was served on a table of new rough boards, covered with a clean table-cloth, around which were arranged benches. Plates, knives and forks, cups and saucers, etc., newly purchased for the trip, were not wanting, and though of the cheapest kind, were yet clean.

The dishes were all placed at once upon the table, but the cook replenished the cups with coffee, and waited upon the table with the promptness and courtesy that should always be found at a first-class hotel, and which add so much to the pleasure of the humblest meal from the humblest board.

"Your fish in these northern regions are very fine," said a large-framed man who sat beside Sydenham, near the head of the table, and seemed to be either a passenger or guest.

"Yes, Doctor, they are, indeed; and this clear, cold, pure water should furnish better fish than the warm and muddy water of the Lower River," said Sydenham.

"And yet we get some good fish in Louisiana," said the person addressed, "and of game as great a variety as you have here."

"You have a far greater variety of game, I think," said Sydenham, laughing; "if you count the alligators and all the different varieties of snakes, *et cetera*, that your swamps can boast of."

"I am too old a hunter," said the Doctor, "not to refuse to go into an enumeration at breakfast, or we would see which side was ahead."

"We can stand it if you can," said one of the men.

"Without making out a catalogue," said Sydenham, "did you know that where we now are is considered to be about the extreme northern limit of the country in which the rattlesnake is found!"

"I did not," said the Doctor, "although my St. Paul friends claim that there are no poisonous reptiles in that vicinity."

"Such is the fact," said Sydenham; "though found in Southern Minnesota and Wisconsin, they are unknown at St. Paul."

"But you have mosquitoes," said the Doctor.

"A few," said Sydenham, "but in point of size and numbers we yield the palm to you."

"I appreciate your generosity in admitting that we of the south, are ahead on snakes and mosquitoes, but which, think you, has produced the most ambitious and unprincipled demagogues?" said the Doctor.

"That is a question not so easily settled by an enumeration of the different species, and a catalogue would be even longer than that we just now proposed to make," said Sydenham.

"It is, after all, a sorrowful subject, and one which we will all have ample time to discuss hereafter," said the Doctor, "for the race of demagogues will never become extinct."

"Yes," said Sydenham, "they are now just what they were two thousand years ago: the bane of republics."

"They correspond exactly with hypocrites in religion," rejoined the Doctor, "and our Saviour has described the one, as the old Greek and Roman writers have the other, as accurately as ever Cuvier or Buffon classified the lower animals. They may almost be known at sight."

"At least their speech or roar will soon betray them," remarked Sydenham.

The raft was now fully in the broad lake, where it is about three miles in width. Lake Pepin is surrounded on all sides by very high bluffs, all crowned with forests, and the scenery throughout its whole extent is very interesting, and in many places beautiful and grand.

As the party rose from the table and walked out upon the deck of their island ship, the sun was just rising over the eastern bluffs, and bathing the lake and valley in a flood of light. The woods and lofty hills cast their shadows along the eastern shore, but the western shore, still fringed with ice, gleamed like a belt of silver. Down the lake to the southeast considerable ice was still in sight, but a channel of open water appeared as far as the eye could reach. Through this, the steamer, a large fine packet boat, held steadily on her way. She was now distant less than one mile, and her lofty chimneys, jack staff, cabin and "Texas," loomed up grandly from the smooth surface of the lake. There was not a breath of wind, and her smoke and steam ascended to a great height in the clear air.

As she neared the raft, the pilot sounded the steam whistle, a kind of double-base and tenor one, making the whole valley and the gorges of the bluffs reverberate with the shrill and startling sound. All had stood silently watching the glorious scenery, and the beautiful gem of art it enclosed, and, as the proud steamer dashed by with the speed of a race-horse, every hat was off, and a cheer went up for the "Northern Belle."

"That," said Sydenham, "is enough to make a man sick of rafting: it is like a train of cars dashing by an old farm wagon."

"In each case, however," said the Doctor, "the spectator enjoys the sight more than those on board."

"I am not so sure of that," said the other, "but your philosophy is the best for us to adopt, for we will have the pleasure or pain of seeing many fine boats pass by us, like a bird by a tortoise, before we reach your State, and I fear you will heartily regret embarking upon a raft."

"I think I can stand it," said the Doctor, "and I can hunt and fish as we go along."

"Yes," said Sydenham, "you can, if you get tired of floating, get off and walk, to rest yourself."

Although the ice was rapidly melting, and very soft and porous, it was still quite thick, and the swell of the steamer had broken off and detached large cakes, that the raftsmen had to avoid by using their sweeps, (that is, large oars,) and by pushing away from them with poles armed with an iron pike at the end. In this way, the day wore on, and, after a day of severe toil, in which all hands were busily engaged, and in which even the Doctor participated, when night came, they had not made more than ten miles. Here, the raft was moored to the shore, at the base of a very steep bluff, some five hundred feet in height, the shore, sides and summit of the bluff being covered with forest.

After sunset the air became quite cold, and the men were glad to put on their coats. Owing to the sluggish current in Lake Pepin, the ice freezes in winter to a great thickness; consequently, in the spring it remains frozen over after the river at St. Paul and above has been open some time, and even when ice has disappeared from the river above and below, thick masses can be found in Lake Pepin.

After supper a large fire was built upon the shore, and around this the men gathered, seated upon logs, or reclining upon blankets or buffalo robes spread upon the ground. Some were playing cards, some were conversing upon various topics, (chiefly rafting or hunting adventures), and others smoked their pipes in silence.

Sydenham and the Doctor sat apart at the base of a high rock, the perpendicular and even surface of which reflected the light and warmth of the fire a few yards in front of it, conversing upon various topics.

The contrast between these two men was very great, and yet there was harmony of opinion and sentiment, and both were honorable and high-souled men. In person, Doctor Ross was of a large frame. In temperament bilious, with something of the nervous, lymphatic and sanguine. Of very dark complexion and black hair, his eyes were blue. His limbs were large and muscular, yet his figure was somewhat loose and ungainly, and his deportment rather careless than awkward. His forehead was high; his features were rather large, and strongly expressive of reflection and deliberation.

His parents had removed from Virginia during the war of 1812, and settled in northern Louisiana, near the Mississippi River, and here Patrick Henry Ross was born.

The Ross family were connected, both by blood and marriage, with that of the great Virginia orator and patriot, and the subject of our sketch inherited not a few of his mental and moral peculiarities, and, in a remarkable degree, that extraordinary foresight, sagacity and prescience of things present and to come, which so distinguished the great Virginian.

But, in all the powers and arts of the orator, Ross, from some inexplicable reason, had never excelled, nor had he, even in this respect, reached the mediocre standing in his own vicinity, which almost every man of any culture was there expected to attain. But he was, and had all his life been, a profound student: of nature, of books, of men, of God's works, and of God's eternal laws. And now, at forty, his mind, after twenty-five years of culture, seemed blossoming into a new stage of existence, and, in its extended flights and fixed and accurate learning, gave promise of one day yielding much wholesome fruit.

Ambition might lure him on more swiftly in the march of life, but could never make him her slave, while for all the petty distinctions of office and political life, he was indifferent.

Yet, in a patriotic desire to see his country go down the great procession of the ages on God's great highway of virtue, truth, and a pure religion, no man excelled him. He followed no man or party, and obeyed the divine injunction, "Put not your trust in princes, nor in any child of man."

With such a man, the political situation of the United States, at the time of which we write, could not fail to excite the most intense solicitude. Sydenham was also deeply interested, though not as yet alarmed. Both had inclined, probably, to the political views of Clay, during the lifetime of that statesman; and the younger, more impulsive and ardent Sydenham, hoped and believed that the principles of Clay, (or rather of the Constitution itself,) if not his particular plans, might triumph through their own inherent force and excellence; but his older and less hopeful companion saw, with great apprehension, the many elements of discord wildly raging through the land, and felt that a young, vigorous and prosperous nation, like ours, full of the life, fire and energy which democratic institutions give, would not bring to the solution of difficult questions that calm analysis of *facts* necessary to establish the TRUTH. Above all, he feared that the great principles of charity, mutual respect between the people of the different parts of this vastly extended country, and kind regard for the interests and feelings of opponents, was almost wanting, or was, at least, *too weak* to exercise a *controlling* influence, and that partisanship and sectionalism would exercise a most baneful effect. This was, in part, the subject of the conversation, continued until nine o'clock, when the two friends, for such they seemed to be rapidly becoming, rose and walked towards the fire, which the men had just deserted for their beds in the rear cabins on the raft.

After standing a few minutes by the half-burned log, against which the fire had been built, they went to the forward cabin, and, lighting a lamp, prepared for bed.

This cabin was about eight feet wide by twelve long, built of rough boards, the sides about five feet high, and the center of the steep, tent-like roof about eight feet in height. In the end towards the front of the raft was a narrow door, and in the rear end a small window set with glass, and made to slide so as to admit air.

A bunk was built in each rear corner, about three feet from the floor, each one being strewn with pine boughs, on which was placed a mattress and blankets. Each bunk was also supplied with a feather pillow, stuffed with the feathers of wild ducks, and on each was also a large buffalo skin, trophies of a hunt on the waters of the Red River of the north. A large bear skin covered the narrow space between the bunks, serving for a rug or carpet. Under the berths were stowed trunks, and on each wall back of the berths, hung a splendid long-range rifle. A couple of double-barreled shot guns stood in the corner. Powder horns, pouches, &c., hung from the walls near the foot of the berths.

Over the door were placed the antlers of a noble buck, while at each end of the room was a small, rude shelf, filled with various articles necessary for a gentleman's toilet, (even on a raft) as well as a few books. Pinned to the walls were a few pencil sketches of landscapes on the upper Mississippi, while most of the remaining surface was covered with various articles of clothing hung upon nails. A small table stood in the corner. There were also three or four camp-stools. On the table lay a plainly bound Bible. There were also one or two magazines and newspapers.

Our friends undressed, kneeled, each by his bunk, and, after a short mental prayer, were soon in bed and asleep.

CHAPTER II.

BY the first grey light of morning, the lines that secured the raft to the shore were cast off, and our party were floating down the lake. The Doctor and one of the men intending to hunt were landed, (after breakfast), by means of the skiff, but at noon were seen on the shore, making signals for the skiff to be sent for them. They were soon taken on board, and reported game scarce, having been unsuccessful. Several wild ducks were, however, shot from the raft, and picked up by sending the skiff for them. Some fish were also caught, the raftsmen keeping hooks constantly "set" for that purpose.

At night, no ice being in sight ahead, and the night clear, Sydenham determined not to "tie up," and the "watches" were arranged accordingly, and the table set for a midnight meal, made ready to serve on short notice. The Doctor had spent the afternoon in reading, while Sydenham had been busy clearing floating cakes of ice. No ice being now in the way, the benches were drawn around the cooking-stove, after supper was over, and the smokers lighted their pipes—the men not on duty going to their beds at once—Sydenham taking the first half of the night, and his pilot the last. Lamps were lighted and placed in suitable positions to notify passing steamers in time to avoid collision. The steersman held for a certain object—the outline of a spur of the bluff far down the lake.

The night was one of remarkable beauty; the moon, now near its full, lighted up the whole heavens, and from the raft the bluffs encircling the lake were in plain view, and the lake itself shone like silver. The least sound was distinctly audible in the perfectly still and serene atmosphere, and the shore echoed back the voices of the men.

Attracted by the remarkable beauty of the scene, Sydenham and his friend left the cabin and paced backward and forward on the slow moving mass. The starry heavens, the beautiful and silent lake, encircled on all sides by the lofty and sombre hills, formed a scene of beauty and grandeur rarely equaled.

The two friends paused and silently gazed on the scene. Almost simultaneously the beautiful words of the psalmist came into their minds and found utterance: "THE HEAVENS DECLARE THE GLORY OF GOD, AND THE FIRMAMENT SHOWETH HIS HANDIWORK."

Save the occasional ripple from the long sweep used in steering, not a sound disturbed the profound stillness. All seemed hushed as though they were floating in mid air.

Suddenly a loud thundering sound, mingled with the crashing of trees and accompanied by a loud report, was heard on the face of the bluff, on the western side of the lake. The earth shook, and a slight tremor was felt in the raft. The echoes of the bluffs took up the sound, and it rang and reverberated far up and down the lake for many seconds, causing the very air to thrill and jar with the mighty sound.

"What is that?" exclaimed the astonished Doctor, all hands rushing out from the cabins as he spoke.

"A mass of rock has become detatched from the cliff

at the summit of the bluff, and fallen or rolled to the bottom," said Sydenham.

"It has produced a fearful noise and vibration," said the Doctor, "such as I do not remember to have ever heard before."

"And well it might," said the other, "for the bluff there is almost perpendicular, and a mass of rock of perhaps ten or twenty tons falling five hundred feet is enough to."

"Do such masses fall often along this lake and river?" said the Doctor, "and have they ever caused loss of life?"

"They fall but seldom," said Sydenham, "and I never knew of any one being hurt by them. But a few miles below where we now are, a house was demolished by a falling rock, not long since, but fortunately it was empty at the time."

"I was once," said a man named Burton, "on a raft that was lying at the foot of a bluff below Winona that came near being smashed, but the stone stopped rolling just a few feet before it got to us; and our old boss swore he had stopped it by throwing his old pipe at it."

"Did he think the pipe was strong enough to stop it?" asked Sydenham.

"I don't know," said Burton, " but it was a very strong pipe; it was only a clay pipe, and he had smoked it four years, and he smoked nearly all the time, except when he was asleep or eating, and he never smoked anything but plug tobacco."

"Perhaps," said one who went by the nickname of "Sandy," "perhaps that was what brought down the rock in the first place, and when it met the pipe it could go no farther."

"I don't know," said Burton, " but the pipe struck the

rock and broke, and the old man was as cross over the loss of it as he would have been if the raft had been smashed, for he had to go nearly a whole day without smoking before he could get another. He almost got crazy—snakes in his boots," he added, by way of explanation.

"You are spinning some tough yarns there," called out Seth Lane, the pilot; "but I knew a little Frenchman who smoked himself into a fit of delirium, if not *delirium tremens.*"

"How is it, Doctor?" asked two or three in a breath, "can a man get *delirium tremens* by smoking?"

"It is possible," said the Doctor, "to get something very near it."

"Do you think smoking injurious?" asked Burton.

"The use of tobacco, whether smoking or chewing, may or may not be injurious," said the Doctor; "it depends upon the constitution and temperament, state of health, &c., of the person using it, and, above all, how it is used, whether in moderation or excess, &c."

"As a general rule, I believe the majority of men who use it would better off without it, and of the remainder, three-fourths use too much, leaving but a small number who are benefitted by it; and yet," said the Doctor, "there is a mystery about tobacco that I do not pretend to fathom fully."

At this point in the discussion a steamer from below hove in sight, and the tobacco question was dropped, Sandy having first remarked that the mystery referred to might serve to account for Burton's pipe story.

Though still at a considerable distance, the sound of the paddle-wheels striking the water could be distinctly heard in the still air, and ere long the whistle broke upon the quiet night, making the lake and lofty hills ring again. Right onward came the good steamer, swiftly rushing over the smooth, deep water, a thing of beauty and of power. She soon passed them, leaving the raft gently rocking in her swell.

All had watched the beautiful sight in silence, and when it was gone the Doctor sighed audibly.

"Think you now that a spectator on a raft enjoys the sight of a passing steamer as much as those on board?" said Sydenham, laughing.

"It all depends upon the state of one's mind," said the Doctor, "if I allow myself to think of the pleasure of travel on an elegant Mississippi steamer (the most pleasant mode of traveling I have ever tried, and one that I believe unequaled) I should soon tire of this; but I had determined to see the great river of *our* country, as travelers see and *feel* the Nile, in a perfectly quiet and tranquil way, with plenty of time for thought, for study and communion with Nature, while floating along the quiet bosom of one of her grandest works."

"I can appreciate your aim," said Sydenham, "and hope you will not be disappointed. I know I have had better thoughts, more true devotion and more *true pleasure* on a much-despised raft than anywhere else. I always carry with me some works of favorite authors, and have read more profitably, here on this river, from the Bible and from all history and poetry, than anywhere else; but never before have I had an appreciative companion, and when I have expressed these thoughts to friends they laughed at the idea; some, no doubt, thinking it affectation on my part."

"The difficulty is," said the Doctor, "that people overlook and despise the great blessings a kind Providence places immediately before them, and seek only the things that are remote and difficult. Had you been a tourist from Europe, come here to view and enjoy the Mississippi and its scenery by floating quietly down it from the falls to the mouth, they would have thought you a devoted lover of Nature, and using wise means for improvement and enjoyment, but as you were engaged in the *business of rafting*, they could not appreciate the other uses of which we speak."

"Naturally enough, too," said Sydenham "for we are apt when in business to be so much absorbed by it as to pay but little attention to other things."

The two friends remained in the glorious night watching the beautiful heavens, the calm lake and its silent shores, until midnight, when, calling Seth Lane, the pilot, Sydenham and his friend retired to their bunks and were soon asleep.

CHAPTER III.

THE sun was up and shining full over the bluffs when our friends were awakened by a call to breakfast. Hastily dressing they stepped out, and dipping up the clear, pure water, performed their morning ablutions.

The raft was now just emerging from the lake and entering the river; the swifter current carrying it along much faster than the day before, and requiring greater care and more labor at the sweeps, both on account of the swifter current and narrower channel.

"Reed's Landing" was soon in sight. This place, a small village, stands at the mouth of the Chippewa River and is a noted resort of raftsmen; the Chippewa being a region of pine, and the seat of a heavy lumbering business. Here Sydenham determined to land; and, as the mode of landing a raft may be new to the reader, we will describe it: To check the "headway" or momentum of such an immense mass as a large Minnesota raft in the swift current of the Mississippi, is an operation that requires considerable skill and prompt decision and action. The raft was steered gradually nearer and nearer to the right bank of the river, until within thirty or forty yards of the shore. The skiff was then brought around to what sailors or boatmen would call the "starboard quarter," that is, the right-hand side of the rear end. Here a huge coil of heavy cable is ready. The skiff is manned by three men, and one end of the cable taken on board. The skiff is now rowed with the greatest possible speed downstream, the cable being payed out by those on the raft; at the call of Sydenham the skiff is landed hastily, and two men spring ashore, and drag the end of the cable coiled in the boat up the bank, and run for a small oak tree, around which they pass one end of the cable, forming "one turn," and this some twenty feet from the end which the men do not fasten, but hold in their hands. The raft has passed them by this time, and soon the strain upon the heavy cable is felt, and it is allowed to yield many feet, but yet strained to almost its capacity. The tremendous friction under this cable (allowed to slip when at so great a tension) causes smoke, and would set it on fire if water was not thrown on. But now the momentum of the raft is checked visibly, now a yielding of two or three feet, and now the raft is "snubbed," and the cable is made "fast" to the tree. The raft now swings close up to the bank, and landing is made complete by means of a heavy plank laid from the raft to the shore.

There were a number of rafts here from the Chippewa, and during the day several more from both rivers came down. Sydenham having laid in necessary stores and made other business arrangements, about the middle of the afternoon gave the orders to "cast off the lines," and soon the huge mass was again floating with the current.

Among raftsmen (strange as it may seem) the same emulation of speed and passing each other exists as among steamboatmen, members of yachting clubs, and owners of fast horses. The fact of their craft being so slow as to make the idea of a race between rafts ludicrous does in no degree diminish their zeal, but rather augments it.

Some rafts float faster than others, and in so piloting them as to save all the distance possible, and also keep where the current is swiftest, there is room for the display of great skill; and there are also, at times, in handling these unwieldy masses, many desperate straits and emergencies requiring the exercise of as great ability as that requisite for the command of the proud ship or steamer. The ship has her sails, the steamer her engines, but the raft must be managed by means of her own weight, the current of the stream, the sweeps, poles and cable. Collisions with other rafts, with steamers and other vessels must be avoided; snags, rocks, shoals and sand-bars must be shunned; the vicissitudes of the weather encountered in rude board shanties; storms and waves encountered without the power of propulsion. These are some of the difficulties and hardships of a vocation of vast importance and benefit to the country, yet but little known to fame. Not a year passes but many a brave man's life is lost on some of the innumerable rafting streams of the United States and Canada, and deeds of daring done that are never heard of outside their own little circle.

There were now a large number of rafts in the river, and the full measure of the excitement of the raftsman's life began to be felt by the men.

Sydenham's mind was engrossed with other thoughts, and he took but little interest in passing or being passed, though anxious for a speedy and safe passage down the river to his destination.

The men, however, were allowed their own way; but Sydenham always insisted that nothing should be done to trespass in the slightest degree upon the rights of others, and that their competitors should always be treated with courtesy. This prevented any of those disgraceful fights and rows which sometimes occur, though less common on the broad Mississippi than on some narrower rivers. As he enjoyed the respect and good-will of those with whom he was acquainted, he was sometimes enabled to prevent difficulties that might become serious, and even fatal, where large numbers of raftsmen were thrown together, and their passions inflamed by whisky. Though not of a very amiable or mild temper, he invariably treated all others with respect, and was always a peace-maker among the men with whom he was thrown. Straightforward, prompt, honorable and decided in speech and action, his courage was of that kind that never deserts the post of duty, though it be the post of danger. The hardy men who follow this vocation have the reputation among some of the people of the river towns, with whom they are brought in contact, of being rude, violent, and given to rowdyism and vice; and, to a superficial observer, this reputation might seem to be deserved. But a closer acquaintance will show that these "manifestations" are due to the peculiarities of the life they lead, and that while men of robust and vigorous frames, plain in speech and manners, yet in them are found as generous and noble qualities as in the more polished denizens of luxurious cities, while their vices, though differently manifested, are no greater in degree than those peculiar to the haunts of wealth and fashion. Like sailors after a long voyage, some raftsmen, after a long period of hardship and exposure, seem to feel recreation to be a necessity, and frequently this takes the form of drunkenness and debauchery; especially is this the case with those who have no families dependent upon them for support, or who do not contemplate marriage. But those who have, or expect to have, wives and homes are disposed almost always to save their money, and shun these vices and temptations; while a few are restrained by religious considerations, or by the virtuous teachings of parents. How often does a period of hardship and constrained self-denial dispose men to yield at once to the allurements of vice. The remedy is to keep the lamp of faith and hope trimmed and brightly burning. Without hope, mankind would be miserable indeed, and evil and worthless as misearble.

CHAPTER IV.

THE change from the lake to the river proper was an agreeable one, as the swift current now hurried them on at greater speed; the river, too, being narrower, brought the towering bluffs closer to the voyagers, and made them appear more grand and lofty. Spring had now advanced sufficiently to clothe the woods, by the river side, in a garb of light, delicate green, and the feathered songsters had appeared by thousands, making the air melodious with their notes.

Showers and thunder storms were now of rather frequent occurrence, but they only added to the beauty and variety of the climate and scenery.

The most delicious fish, bass, pike, pickerel, &c., were caught in abundance, and cooked in various ways. Fresh butter, milk, eggs, &c., were to be had at the various landing places, together with stores of all kinds, so that all fared sumptuously every day.

The delightful climate of Minnesota has been the theme of many a tongue and pen, but never can it be more enjoyed than on its great river in spring and summer. The air is clear, pure and exhilerating, free from that *humidity*, so common in the eastern States. The showers and rain storms are usually of short duration, and when they are over, clear off at once, leaving the atmosphere more balmy and delightful than before. The long, dreary periods of rainy, cloudy weather, so common in most of the States, are here almost unknown. The skies are usually cloudless, and both nights and days are brilliant and glorious. Throughout most of the States of the great valley of the Mississippi, the nights, during the summer, are quite warm; but in Minnesota and Wisconsin, the nights are cool, giving refreshing sleep, and keeping the system constantly braced up and vigorous.

Our voyagers were in excellent health and spirits, and the men were full of cheerful gaiety, even when their duties were most arduous and laborious.

The pretty towns they were passing were busy with the full press of the spring trade, now fairly opened. At every landing place, barges were loading with wheat (Minnesota's great staple) and steamers were descending the river to LaCrosse, Prairie du Chien, and other points, with large "tows" of loaded barges, and returning with the same empty, or freighted in part with merchandise, groceries, farming implements, harvesting machines, &c.

The surplus wheat product of Minnesota and western Wisconsin is—or was at the time of our story—collected chiefly at the towns along the Mississippi, and shipped thence, in bulk, to La Crosse and other railroad termini lower down, in large barges, towed by steamers. From these barges, it is transferred by steam elevators to cars carrying about ten tons each, and forwarded to Milwaukee and Chicago. Large quantities are also shipped down the river to St. Louis, and some to New Orleans for export.

The river was now cheerful with the excitement of commerce and travel, and beautiful in the warmth and verdure of the genial spring.

Sydenham's duties were arduous, as they now floated day and night; but the Doctor seemed to enjoy, to the full, the beauty of the glorious days and starlit nights.

While almost constantly in sight of steamers or towns,

glowing with the warm active energy of commerce, he was yet floating quietly on the silent river, and enjoying all the tranquil beauties of nature as much as though he were exploring for the first time an undiscovered country, the streams, hills and landmarks of which were yet waiting to receive their names. And here we will remark that very many of the localities of the upper Mississippi retain the names given them by the early French explorers, while not a few retain the original Indian names.

On the lower river this is not so much the case. There the bends, islands, &c., have usually been named by the American pilots, while most of the towns have been named by the early French or American settlers, in some cases adopting names of places in ancient Egypt, France and Spain.

The third day after leaving Reeds Landing was Sunday, and Sydenham, according to his invariable custom, laid by at midnight of Saturday night, near a place known as Grey Eagle's Cave.

CHAPTER V.

WE have said that our party had laid by for the Sabbath near a noted cave. This cave was known among the river men as the abode of an old hermit Sioux chief. It is not uncommon for the traveller on the upper Mississippi to see Indians on the river, in their canoes though their tribes have long since moved west. But there is NO GREAT AND BEAUTIFUL RIVER like this in their new home, and they seem reluctant to part forever from its clear, sweet waters, so long their own, ere the white man came in his power and greed to drive them away.

Grey Eagle had been a noted chief in his day—famed throughout the entire Sioux and neighboring nations—and had known prosperity and power as a ruler and leader. But misfortune had pursued him. His seven sons had either died or perished in battle. He had outlived his wives, brothers and sisters. His parents had long since passed away. He had no near relative living; his sons had left no offspring. Lonely and stricken in years, when his tribe moved away from their old homes, he remained, saying that he wished to die near the great river. He had been to St. Paul frequently, and received an annuity regularly from the government. He had, many years ago, listened to the teachings of a good missionary, and had been converted and baptized in the Catholic Church.

At the point where our party moored their raft, the river makes a bend to the left. Here the channel is close to the Wisconsin shore, while opposite, on the Minnesota side, is quite a wide expanse of water, a kind of bay, with but little current. From the river bank, in the "bight" of the bay, back to the foot of the bluff, is about three-fourths of a mile covered with a heavy forest, and is a favorite resort of deer.

Back through the hills, a ravine or small valley, drained by a fine trout brook, opens up from the large river valley. To the left of this rises a lofty peak, surmounted by a large dome-shaped rock, plainly visible up and down the river for many miles, and known as Grey Eagle's Tower.

On the side of the bluff, about two hundred feet above the valley, is the cave, and just below this, a few rods up the little valley near the bank of the stream, in a beautiful and sheltered nook remote from any white man's abode, stood the lodge of the hermit chief. From his lodge a zigzag path led up the steep side of the bluff to the entrance to the cave, which opened to the east, and commanded at all seasons of the year a full view of the rising sun. From the cave the path led by a circuitous route to the summit. Here Grey Eagle would often sit for hours, his eyes fixed upon the river and the steamers—the life and commerce borne upon its tide. The cave was his place of worship, and here, morning and evening, his orisons were offered up. It consisted of an outer room about ten feet in width, twelve feet in height and fifteen in length, with an entrance about eight feet each way. From this room a passage about three feet in width led back into the bluff about one hundred feet to another room, larger than the first, and dark except at sunrise or just after, when for a short time it would be light enough to see objects dimly; but, at the winter solstice, the direction of the narrow passage was such, that at the moment the sun was just above the horizon, its beams poured full into the inner chamber, and were reflected from the white walls and stalactites with dazzling effulgence. From the inner room a very narrow and difficult passage led still farther into the bluff; but it had never been explored by white men, and if the Indians had, they would not impart any information concerning it. Their traditions declared that far in the very heart of the bluff, under the summit of the dome, rested the bones of a great chief, the favorite of the Great Spirit, who died many hundred moons before the first white man was seen upon the Mississippi, and that a dreadful fate would overtake any who should penetrate these hidden recesses to disturb his remains. The cave itself was held sacred and believed by some to be the abode of the Great Spirit. Others believed that he only visited it at that time of the year, when the sun's rays, at his command, penetrated to the inner chamber and made it glorious while he remained.

Pilgrimages were made to the cave at all seasons, but the most sacred period was the winter solstice. None then presumed to enter the inner chamber save after long preparation by fasting and penance. They then entered before sunrise, and, while there, remained prostrate on their faces, silent and motionless.

In this climate a cloudy day or sunrise is not common at this season, and it is very rare indeed to have successive mornings without a bright sunrise. Should there come a season, however, when the sun's rays did not enter the inner chamber of the cave at all, by reason of clouds, it was viewed as an omen of evil, and of the anger of the Great Spirit. Just before the white men came, their traditions relate that this occurred for three seasons in succession; and they believe that in a future period a time will come again when three winters will pass in which no sunshine will enter the inner chamber of the sacred cave, and, after that, great calamities will fall upon the *white* race.

At the time of which we write, there were but few Indians in the vicinity; yet no winter passed in which, at the sacred season, there were not some devotees prostrate in the silent vault, gladdened annually by the rays of the December sun.

Grey Eagle was a devout christian; but no pilgrim visited the cave who was as strict in this singular worship as himself. He insisted that he could in this way keep holy the Christmas season, that the God of the white man was the Great Spirit of the Indian, and that the cave was the Indian's church. White men, he said, worshipped in their churches at *Christmas*; why should not he, an Indian, worship in this cave at the Indian's Christmas. The good priest, finding that there were no traces of sun worship in these rites, made no further opposition, but hung the sacred symbol of the church on the walls of both outer and inner rooms, and on one occasion held mass in the outer room, and explained to the poor, naked children of the woods what Christmas meant. Grey Eagle firmly believed that there was a direct connection between the sacred season of the Indians and the Christmas of the white men.

The good missionary viewed the coincidence with awe and wonder, and saw in it an innocent means of gaining the affections of these poor people to the pure and perfect religion of Christ. And the transition is easy, for never, on this earth, have any people, without the aid of divine revelation, attained to so pure a religion as the unlettered

North American Indian. Being uninstructed in the christian principles of mercy and forgiveness, they are sanguinary and revengeful, but Pagans they are not in in any sense, and idol worship is unknown among them. Compare the noble creed of the untutored Indian, of a Supreme Being, and of immortal life beyond this world, with the horrible and bloody fanaticism of India, the stupid idolatry of China, the beastly and inhuman diabolism of Africa, or even with the creeds of the learned and powerful nations of antiquity: Carthage, Rome, Greece and Egypt, Assyria and Persia; and how sublimely it rises before us in its simple beauty and grandeur.

A Great Good Spirit; an immortal future of happiness for the just and brave—these are the grand ideas eliminated by the Indian, and placed on a height above all forms and systems of idolatry of every age and clime; above the Aztecs and Peruvians, with their altars reeking with human gore; above the mythology of Homer and Virgil; above the curious creed of the men who built the Pyramids, and their sacred cats and crocodiles; above the misbelieving Jews, continually relapsing into idolatry, and worshipping beastly images even at the foot of Sinai; and, with shame may we ask, above how many of the false and foolish ones who have perverted Christ's gospel, from the time he stood on the mount to the present hour. Whatever may be said of the Indian's cruelty in war, he has been noble in this, that he does not enshrine Deity in beasts, or images, or monsters, or sun, or fire.

Well might the devoted French missionaries of early days desire to convert, and promote the welfare of such a race. All honor to those kind, noble and enterprising Frenchmen; those devoted and gallant christians.

CHAPTER VI.

THE Sabbath morning sun rose beautifully clear, and, though some clouds in the west and south betokened a storm, yet our two friends prepared to pay a visit to Grey Eagle, to the cave and to the peak above it.

The fatigue of the past few days, and the night watches, caused all to sleep late except the Doctor, who, having had nothing to do, rose early, and with a spy glass made a careful examination of what he supposed the locality of the cave, from the description Sydenham had given him the day previous. He soon, however, laid down his glass, and, shoving a plank out to the shore, he landed and started out for a morning walk on the soil of Wisconsin. After an hour's ramble he returned, and found all hands up and breakfast nearly ready. Sydenham invited him to read prayers, which he did from his Episcopal prayer-book, together with a selection from the Psalms. They then sat down to an excellent breakfast of fresh fish from the river, cooked admirably, boiled potatoes, baked potatoes, fried pork, sour kraut, bread, butter, cakes, crackers and excellent coffee. After breakfast some articles were put up that could not fail to be acceptable to the poor and lonely old man. A stout bag was procured, and in this Sydenham placed a small quantity of coffee, sugar, tea, tobacco, bread, crackers, matches, powder, lead, etc. In another bag some flour was provided; in another, meal sifted and ready for use. The doctor produced a bottle of wine and a New York pictorial newspaper. These articles were all placed in the bow of the skiff, and the friends entered. The Doctor took the oars, and Sydenham took a seat in the stern and steered for the opposite shore, about three-quarters of a mile distant. They were at first obliged to contend with a very swift current, where the river swept around the bend, but, once out of this, the current in the wide expanse between the channel and the Minnesota side was very gentle, and they soon reached the shore. Here they moored their skiff in a little cove at the extreme terminus of the crescent-shaped bay, and chained it securely to a small willow tree. Then dividing the weight to be carried between them, they set out for the bluff. Their way at first led through tangled thickets and some sedgy miry ground, and they were obliged to make a considerable detour to get upon ground firm enough to bear them. At length they came to the little brook which they supposed flowed from the little valley. Crossing this on a small log, they soon came to a deer path which they supposed led up the valley or ravine. Nor were they mistaken, for ere long the barking of a dog announced that they were approaching some human habitation, and soon they came in sight of a small lodge made of skins. As we have said, this stood a little way up the valley that opened out of the bottom-land of the river. The land, however, was higher even at the very entrance of the narrow valley, by several feet, and the soil was more mixed with gravel and the fragments of stone. The brook had here some rapids and one perpendicular fall of about two feet into a deep pool—a fine trout hole. About one hundred yards above this, on a little knoll two or three feet above the level of the surrounding land, stood Grey Eagle's lodge.

The little valley at this point was about two hundred yards in width, dotted with scattering oaks, and, on the right-hand side the brook as you go up the valley, a heavy undergrowth of thickets; but the space on the left-hand side was mostly open and free from brushwood. The brook ran nearly through the center of the valley opposite the lodge, but at other places curved from side to side, laving the base of the lofty hills on each side. The valley grew gradually narrower back from the river, until, at the distance of three-fourths of a mile, it came to an end, or rather dwindled to a mere ravine, with steep sides, at the bottom of which swiftly coursed the brook, entering the heart of the valley by a perpendicular fall of about fourteen feet.

The valley was a favorite resort for game at all seasons of the year; and Grey Eagle had little trouble in supplying himself with meat, while fish, he said, swam up to his door, the little knoll where the lodge stood being only about thirty feet from the water.

On one side the lodge, at the distance of perhaps fifteen paces, stood a large oak, near the root of which, under a projecting rock, bubbled a beautiful spring. The lodge was made of dressed deer skins sewed together and stretched over poles, circular in form, and about twelve feet in diameter at the ground.

The barking of his dog aroused the chief from a dreamy reverie, and he came out to see the cause.

Sydenham, who had some knowledge of Indian manners, made a friendly salutation, which was returned by Grey Eagle, who then in pretty good English invited them to enter. He was a man of about six feet in height, and rather slender, his features looking almost emaciated. The erect form of the Indian has become proverbial, but the tall form of Grey Eagle, from the weight of years and sorrow, was a little bent. His face, while rigid with the stoical indifference so characteristically Indian, was yet softened by a pensive sadness, and his deep-set and piercing eyes looked kindly upon his guests, whom he saw at once were not prompted by the same motives as most of those who came to see him.

Sydenham and the Doctor took their seats upon a bear-skin which he spread for them. The Doctor produced his tobacco pouch and passed it to the chief, who took it with an Indian expression of satisfaction, and, after filling his pipe, passed it to Sydenham. Their pipes were soon lighted, and all smoked for a time in silence. At length Grey Eagle enquired if they "came from steamboat."

"No," said Sydenham, "we came from St. Croix with lumber raft," and he pointed to where the raft lay.

"Ugh!" was all the reply Grey Eagle made, and all smoked on in silence. At length the Doctor spoke:

"Why does Grey Eagle live here alone when his tribe have gone away?"

"Grey Eagle is not living but dying," replied the Indian, and he extended his shrunken hand and arm, and then bared his breast, withered, and seamed with a deep scar. "Grey Eagle's fathers, and his wives and children, died near the Great River, and so must he if the white man will let him," and he looked enquiringly at the Doctor.

"Surely, no one will disturb you," said the Doctor, "for you would not harm them."

"Grey Eagle has fought the Chippewas, but he has never shed white man's blood: they have wronged him, but he loves the good missionary."

"But you are all alone here," said the Doctor.

"No," said the Indian, "all around in these hills and

valleys sleep those Grey Eagle loved, and the Great Spirit whispers to him in the winds, and speaks to him in the thunder. Grey Eagle's fathers always believed in the Great, Good Spirit, and he believes in Jesus Christ, too, and he loves both." And he bowed his head reverently.

Neither the Doctor nor Sydenham made any reply, but mused in silence.

The clouds had been gathering all the morning, and now overspread the whole heavens. While they sat silently musing upon the words of the old chief, a peal of thunder, long, loud and deep, rolled across the firmament and died away in the distance.

Grey Eagle took his pipe from his lips, clasped his hands and bowed his head.

Soon it ceased, and he rose to his feet, his eye kindled, and his form dilated. "No," he said, "the white man will have all the lands, the river, the hills, valleys and pararie; the trees, the little creeks, and the lakes, the fish, the deer, the bear, all the grass, the rocks—everything. If the Indian gives them all, they will let him die in peace, or the Great Spirit will punish them, for he watches over his red children as well as the white. Your great book tells you that not even a little bird falls to the ground without his knowledge, and that he not only listens to all that we say, but knows all that we think. The red man does not talk as much as the white, but he will hear him." The poor Indian sank upon the ground, while his whole form quivered with emotion.

Again the thunders pealed across the heavens, louder, sharper, fiercer than before. The terrific sound crashed through the narrow valley like the discharge of a hundred pieces of artillery. It was accompanied by a blinding flash, lurid and awful beyond anything that either Sydenham or the Doctor had seen.

The Indian bowed his head to the earth, his lips moved, his limbs trembled, and his heaving breast showed the deep emotion that convulsed his soul. Not a word was uttered for some moments. Sydenham and his friend also bowed their heads in silent devotion. At length the chief rose to his feet, extended one hand to each of the white men, and clasped theirs warmly.

"You," he said, "are good white men."

"Our red brother is our friend," said Sydenham, "and God is the Father of us all."

"The young elk loves the high ground, but the skunk loves the swamp," said the Indian.

The rain now began to fall in torrents, but the skins of which the lodge was made were dressed in such a way as to shed the water very well; a little came through the hole at the top, and hissed upon the embers of the morning fire. Grey Eagle produced a few dry sticks, laid them upon the fire and kindled a blaze, thus removing the chilling influences of the storm which raged without.

Sydenham and the Doctor now had time to observe the good order and neatness of the wigwam. Grey Eagle was also cleanly in his person, and his dress was made of neatly dressed deer-skin.

"Have they ever molested you here, or wanted to drive you off?" said the Doctor at length.

"Yes," said Grey Eagle, "land-hunters and deer-hunters have come here, and ate my meat and fish, slept in my lodge, and then told me I had no business here, that this was now the white man's land, and that I ought to go west."

"Have you ever talked with the agent at St. Paul about it?" enquired Sydenham.

"Grey Eagle should not ask leave of any white man to stay here," said the Chief; "but I have asked the agent at St. Paul, and he said I must go west. I told him I was the last of my blood and would soon die, and wanted to die here. He said then I had better *buy* the land at the land office, or some white man might, and give me trouble. I told him that as the red men had owned it all, they might let one old man stay here until he died, and then give him back land enough for his grave, and I asked him to give me a paper to show the white men that came to my camp. He said it would do no good if any one came who claimed the land, and that I had better buy it. I told him I had no money, and was too old to make any by trapping. He said my tribe could pay for it out of their annuities. I told him my tribe were very poor, and needed more than their annuity. He then said he would do all he could for me; he would talk to the river men about me, and he did not think any one would ever be mean enough to trouble me, and the good missionary said so too; and most of the white men have been good. Steamboatmen gave me many presents—bread and flour; and I gave them trout. I rode on steamboat to St. Paul, and one good lady gave me this," (and he produced a handsome Bible)—"but books are not good for Indians. Another gave me this," and he showed them a small ivory cross; "another one this," and he showed them a small pair of shears. "But my white brothers are hungry, and Grey Eagle will feed them."

The chief accordingly set about and prepared some dried venison, while Sydenham produced the articles they brought for him, which were recived by Grey Eagle with an expression of gratitude and satisfaction. The lodge contained several tin cups, plates, etc., and the Doctor found a small kettle in which he prepared some coffee, of which the Indian was very fond.

Soon all were partaking of a comfortable repast, which might be said to bear some relation to both civilized and savage life. The common opinion that the Indian modes of cooking are all rude and filthy may be correct in many cases; yet their mode of roasting and baking meats, &c., are not to be despised, and many epicures accustomed to the most delicate and refined processess of the art of cooking have pronounced birds roasted in the ashes by Indians superior to anything they had ever eaten.

By the time dinner was over the rain had entirely ceased, and the sun was shining. The pipes were again lighted, and, after smoking a few minutes in silence, the Doctor made inquiry of Grey Eagle in regard to the cave, its history, &c. As we have already given this, it need not be repeated.

Both the Doctor and Sydenham expressed a desire to see it, and the chief offered to guide them. They accordingly set out, having first prepared a torch to light when they had entered it.

The way was steep, and so slippery from the rain, that even Sydenham and the Doctor found the ascent very toilsome. The old Indian complained of feebleness, and moved with difficulty up the ascent.

When half-way up they paused to rest, and the old man sat down. "When Grey Eagle was young," he said, "he could go up such a hill like the deer, but now he could only creep like the tortoise."

As they neared the cave, Grey Eagle observed that a solitary tree that stood near the entrance (the only one for some rods around) had been riven by the lightning.

"Oh," said the Doctor, "I thought that must have struck near, and so it did."

"Yes," said Sydenham, "it was terrific; I never heard such thunder in Minnessota before."

The old Indian groaned audibly, and pointed his withered hand toward it. "That," said he, "was Grey Eagle's tree; it is gone, and death will soon strike Grey Eagle."

It was an oak of beautiful shape, though somewhat knotty and stunted. Yet it had adorned the rough hillside, and its round and symmetrical top had been an object of beauty, visible for a great distance, and from the decks of passing steamers many a glass had been leveled at it as marking the entrance to the cave.

The white men tried to console the chief, but he uttered not a word.

The two friends looked off on the river. Two large steamers were in sight, one bound up, the other down. The Indian heard the boats and raised his head and gazed long and earnestly upon them At length he rose and led the way into the cave. After pausing a few minutes to examine the first room, and the rude carving upon its walls, they groped their way back through the long narrow passage to the inner chamber. Here was darkness. Sydenham produced some matches and lighted the torch. In a moment a beautiful sight burst upon them. The walls were remarkably smooth and even, and almost pertectly white. The roof was arched, and from it depended numerous stalactites that shown in the light of the torch like silver.

On the north wall hung a small wooden cross, placed there, as we have said, by the missionary. Grey Eagle moved toward it and kneeled with his hands upon his forehead for some minutes, while Sydenham and the Doctor removed their hats and bowed their heads reverently.

"What a beautiful chapel," said the Doctor.

"Beautiful, indeed," replied Sydenham, "and I marvel not that the good Father Martel saw fit to use it as such, for, were the ascent to it less difficult, nothing better could be desired."

The floor was as smooth and even as the walls, and the air of the cave seemed perfectly pure. On the west was the crevice that was supposed by some of the Indians to lead to the tomb of "Great Buffalo," the famed chief of ancient days.

Grey Eagle, when interrogated, seemed reluctant to converse upon the subject. He, however, thrust the torch into the crevice, lighting it up for many yards, and they could see that for a considerable distance, at least, it did not enlarge, and, as they were not prepared to attempt its exploration, and as their kind host evidently did not wish them to do so, the friends contented themselves with enjoying for half an hour the beauties of the inner chamber.

Leaving the cave, they determined not to ascend to the summit of the peak, as both were fond of a quiet Sunday, and had already encroached upon its hours of rest more than their wont. Descending the hill, they bade Grey Eagle a kind and respectful good-bye.

The old chief seemed touched, and held their hands in his as though they had always been his friends, and he would never see them again. Alas! little did either of the party think how soon they would see him again, and under what changed circumstances. But the events that took place at Grey Eagle's lodge after the departure of our two friends must form the subject of another chapter.

CHAPTER VII.

ON the same day on which the men from the raft visited Grey Eagle, a common two-horse wagon, such as those used by farmers in the west for hauling may have been seen on the road that led down the river valley. It was drawn by two horses, and in it were three men.

One of these was a hunter and wood-chopper named Bill Smith, whose cabin stood on the river bank, about six miles above Grey Eagle's lodge; another was the surveyor of the county, named Farley; the third was a burly farmer from Wisconsin, who had come out to buy land, and was strongly impregnated with that "Anglo Saxon propensity"—*to get land*. His name was George Brown; and he was one of that class of men never troubled with hesitation of purpose, or conscientious doubts as to the rightfulness of any course of action which he had once decided upon. Generally honest (in his way), and occasionally benevolent, he was yet arbitrary and unscrupulous in matters that affected his pecuniary interests, whenever he thought he had the law on his side, this being the standard that usually guided him. Being a man of powerful frame and very passionate, he was frequently disposed to resort to violence, and was more feared than loved by those who knew him.

The hunter was a man who hated all Indians, and thought they ought to be exterminated, or at least driven away. Toward them he had no conscience, and thought if he could buy an otter skin worth five dollars of an Indian for a quart of flour it was all right. Yet he was not a bad man in his intercourse with whites, and was esteemed by many as quite an honest, kind, worthy man. He seemed to have "two consciences—one for white men and one for Indians."

The county surveyor being an officer elected by the people, had long since learned to so shape his course as to suit the largest number of people. Popularity he regarded not only as the sure and only road to office, but as the highest evidence of the excellence of a man's character, and the correctness of his conduct—and really a great virtue in itself. Being a popular man, he was therefore a complacent, self-satisfied man; never disputed with any one, but smiled benignantly upon himself and all the world in general, except political opponents. These he respected greatly, if in a majority, but if a minority, he viewed them with as much malevolence as could be expected from a mild man who never got in a passion.

Here, then, we have the party who were *en-route* for Grey Eagle's lodge. Brown had entered the land at the United States Land Office at St. Paul, and was now going to see it. He had engaged the surveyor to survey it, and Bill Smith to guide them through the woods, carry the chain, &c.

We will now return to the lodge. After Sydenham's return to the raft, and the men heard of the cave, &c., they started in a body to look at it. On arriving at the foot of the bluff, they were troubled to find the path, and went to Grey Eagle's lodge. As soon as the old chief found they were from the raft of the "Young Elk," as he called Sydenham, he went with them and showed them the cave, and explained to them its wonders and traditions.

This party had just gone, and the old man, fatigued with the repeated ascent of the steep bluff, was stretched at full length on his pallet of bear-skins, and was in that dreamy state peculiar to age, when the wagon reached the entrance to the little valley, and Brown, accompanied by Bill Smith, started up the "hollow" in search of the "Indian squatter," as he called Grey Eagle, of whom, and his peculiarities, habits, &c., Smith had given him a lengthy account, colored and exaggerated, as might be expected, from an Indian hater; and he verily believed that there was a vast amount of evil within the wrinkled and shrunken hide of the old hermit. He had heard of the Indian belief in regard to the cave; and these stories, exaggerated and distorted in a hundred different ways, had been rich food for his ignorant and superstitious nature. He believed the poor, dried-up old Indian held direct communication with the Devil, and that the cave was the place of their meeting. He had often longed to visit the cave, but dared not do so. Once, indeed, in company with another hunter, who was equally superstitious, he had entered the outer room. Here, with palpitating hearts, they began examining the strange, rude carving on the walls, when the sound of a voice from the recesses of the cave reached their ears. Heretofore they had thought that midnight was the hour at which old Nick came up from below, to fill his appointments with Grey Eagle; but the instant they heard the strange sounds from the interior of the cavern, they knew at once that Satan was there in person. Grasping their rifles, they started down the hill on a full run; nor did they pause a moment until, far away and breathless, they paused and peered back through the gloomy and solemn woods, to see if pursuit was made. They could see nothing suspicious, but both fancied they smelt sulphur or gunpowder, they could not tell exactly which. For some time after this, Smith complained of soreness and stiffness in his joints, and thought it some spell that the old Indian necromancer had laid on him. His wife, however, did not believe the Devil was in that part of the country, and that the soreness was caused by running and jumping down such a steep hillside. She even expressed surprise "that he hadn't driv his legs up into his body." Long experience had convinced her that most of the ills and mishaps that befell her husband were caused by whisky; and she hinted that it was so in this case; an insinuation that greatly exasperated the usually good-natured husband.

Both hunters, too, complained that their rifles would not shoot "worth a cuss," after this, and were in serious trouble on that account, until they met an aged man who hunted in Kentucky in very early times, when witches were about, who assured them that a spell had been laid upon their rifles by some witch or wizard, probably by Grey Eagle, and that a sure remedy was to shoot out of each a silver bullet. An old Spanish dollar was accordingly procured and melted; the bullets moulded, fired from the guns, and all was right again. This remarkable proof convinced even the good woman, who never again disputed the point with her husband about the old chief's dealings with Satan. Still she looked with more dread to his visits to the neighboring village than to his occasional meeting with the old Indian in the woods. Whenever this happened, Bill scowled upon the chief with no friendly expression, and Grey Eagle passed on in quiet indifference.

All this, and more, Bill had related to Brown, who listened incredulously and remarked that he would not let any of the Devil's imps stay on his land; that he was not afraid of them, even if old Nick was there in person. He would show them who owned that land. With this bravado they approached the poor hovel on the little knoll.

The dog was lying basking in the sun, and, at the sound of approaching footsteps, sprang up and ran towards them barking fiercely. Brown took up a stone and threw it at the dog. It struck him on the shoulder, and the poor beast limped yelling into the lodge.

Grey Eagle roused himself from his couch and sat up. Just then the the burly form of Brown with Bill Smith at his back entered the lodge.

"Hello!" said he to Grey Eagle, gruffly, "what are you doing here?"

The chief rose with dignity. "Grey Eagle harms no one, and is the white man's friend," he said calmly. "Why do you hurt my dog?"

"Because I don't l ke dogs or Indians," said the invading ruffian, "as you will find out."

The chief's eye flashed fire, but he stood motionless as a statue. At length he subdued his anger and spoke.

"The dog is the Indian's friend; he would not hurt you, nor would I. No white man has ever been turned away from Grey Eagle's lodge. The sun is going down, and the night wind is cold: stay in Grey Eagle's lodge and eat his venison."

There is an antagonism between good and evil. There is also an attraction and repulsion of good and evil impulses in the continuous action and reaction of the human mind. Brown had only seen, heretofore, the most degraded of the Indians, who occasionally lounged about the towns of Wisconsin, whom he looked upon as pilfering vagabonds. He had approached the lodge with the idea of his own importance, and the utter worthlessness of the old Indian, who would not go west. As the chief stood before him and spoke, there was that in his eye and bearing which changed all this in an instant. He felt that he had been wrong, that he had done wrong, and there, as the old man proffered hospitality in return for his rudeness and violence, he felt at first almost ashamed. But the calm dignity of the chief was a keener rebuke than he could endure. It nettled him, and touched him in his sorest and meanest point. The chief had shown magnanimity, and this called for a like return. Brown could not give a proper return, for magnanimity formed no part of his nature. And so the evil impulse predominated, and his answer was what might have been expected.

"I am not beholden to you or any other red skin for lodgings or food," he said. "I own this place. I have bought it and paid for it. The land is mine, and the law would give me this lodge if I wanted it; but perhaps I will let you take it away if you will behave yourself. But I shall use it while I want it," he added.

The old man heard the beginning of this cruel speech with an expression of contempt upon his countenance; as it proceeded, this changed to one of deep grief, and when it concluded he fell back with a low moan. "Great Spirit," he said, "help the poor Indian." He had borne wounds and torture, but this was too much.

From the time the two white men had entered the lodge the dog had remained in a remote corner out of sight, giving occasionally a low whine of pain or growl of anger. He had watched the face of his master and of the invaders alternately. The strange sympathy and knowledge of his race seemed at fault as to whether they were friends or enemies— or whether his old master would have to fight or surrender. Brown (as we have said) was a large, powerful man, and in the habit of speaking in a loud, rough tone, and gesticulating in rather a threatening manner, He did so on this occasion in announcing to the astonished old Indian his rights of ownership. The animal watched every motion intently, and when his old master fell back with a cry of despair, the poor little lame dog seemed to conclude that the time for action had arrived. He flew at Brown with great energy, and fastened his teeth in his boot-leg. That worthy was afraid of dogs, and started back at first with an exclamation of fright. He soon saw, however, that the dog was small, and the leather of his boot-legs very heavy. The chances of battle were, therefore, immensely in his favor. His rage was roused to a fearful pitch, and he at once determined to annihilate the enemy. He seized him with both hands, and placed him under his feet preparatory to stamping him to death with his heavy boots.

The old Indian revived. He saw the danger of his four-footed companion. He rushed to drag him from under the foot of the giant. Brown's blood was up. He struck the old man a tremendous blow that felled him senseless to the earth. In doing so the dog escaped. Brown turned again to the Indian. He saw that he was prostrate and insensible, and that he could stamp him with his heavy boots. He at first thought of doing so, but concluded he would not. He contented himself with dragging the insensible body out of the lodge to the side of the knoll. His anger then cooled; there was nothing to oppose him. His eye rested on Bill Smith, who stood looking on with amazement. The current of that individuals thoughts had turned. What he had witnessed in ten minutes had undone the fixed prejudices and opinions of years. He was not entirely destitute of common-sense, and he had human feelings. He heard the Indian call upon his Maker in his grief, and this had shaken his faith in his being in league with the Devil. Indeed, he began to think that if the Devil was about, he had entered into the person of Brown. The little black dog that he had always supposed to be the familiar of the Indian wizard he saw was a perfectly natural dog, and not at all supernatural; and he immediately liked and pitied the little creature. When he saw the prostrate and bleeding form of the old Indian, he remembered for the first time for years favors granted him by Grey Eagle when he first came to the country, before any towns were built; and a twinge of remorse and pity shot through him. So, when Brown looked around for the hunter's approval, he saw a very different expression from what he had expected.

"I have cleaned out your Devil's brood," he said.

"You did a big thing, Captain," said Bill, who immediately brought water from the spring and bathed the Indian's head, wrists and breast. As he did so, he saw the deep scar that seamed it. This at once exploded another crotchet of his absurd superstition—his belief in the invulnerability of Grey Eagle, through the evil power which he supposed he possessed. He bathed the old man's head for some time, and then poured a little whisky down his throat. The chief opened his eyes at length, and stared wildly about him. Soon memory brought back to him the recollection of all that had passed, and his mind at once connected Bill Smith with the outrage done him, equally with Brown. He did not speak, but motioned him away. Smith drew back: slowly and with difficulty the feeble man sat up and leaned his head on his hands. Brown felt relieved at this, for he did not want any danger impending over him of a chance of being tried for murder—if the killing of an Indian would be accounted murder, or noticed.

At length the old man rose to his feet. Brown and Smith both felt relieved, for both had feared that from his age and feebleness he might not recover, but die where he lay. When he walked away, therefore, this little shade of anxiety was removed.

The surveyor now came up and joined them. Brown produced a flask of whisky and tendered it to Smith. The hunter drank deeply, and soon all his old hate for the Indians returned. Brown proceeded to relate to the surveyor all that had passed, stating that the Indian had been insolent to him, and when the dog attacked him he came on to the help of the dog in assaulting him; and he had "cleaned them out."

"Good enough for him," said the surveyor; "served him right."

Bill Smith heard this, and knew its incorrectness, but the spark of manly honor in him was not strong enough to cause him to come out at once and maintain the truth against a man like Brown. Indeed, as the liquor began to have more effect upon him, and as he came more under the influence of the strong-willed Brown, he joined in the conversation and endorsed all that was said, denouncing Grey Eagle and all Indians with many an oath.

Securing their horses for the night, and feeding them in the wagon-bed or box, they began to prepare supper, using partly articles brought with them and partly those found in the lodge. After supper the property in the lodge was overhauled and examined, and speculations indulged in as to whether the Indian would ever come back to claim it. All concluded that Brown could claim and hold the lodge, the poles being firmly set in the earth. Bill Smith examined the rifle critically. It was beautifully mounted with silver, and the stock was handsomely carved. On one side was an eagle with wings extended; on the other the same bird at rest. There was also a steamboat and a log house. Bill examined all this with delight. He knew its great range and accuracy, and he longed to possess it. The powder horn and flask were also elaborately wrought, and stained with great skill. The belt, hunting knife, tomahawk, etc., were all overhauled and examined. So were all the little presents the chief had received. The surveyor gave his particular attention to the skins and robes that formed the bed—these were the articles that *he* coveted. The flask was circulated again, and the probability of Grey Eagle's whereabouts was discussed, and the danger of his seeking revenge that very night when they were all asleep.

"But," said Bill Smith, "he has no weapons."

"No matter," said Brown; "he might slip in and get them."

"Yes," said Farley, "if we slept soundly he might come back and kill us all."

It soon became the settled conviction of all that they were not safe while the Indian was about.

"Even if he went west," they said, "he might still plan some revenge." Soon they all agreed in wishing him dead, and a regret was expressed that he had not been killed. At length it was agreed that they should keep watch that night, each one taking his turn. Smith agreed to take the first part of the night. Brown and Farley then lay down in Grey Eagle's bed of skins. So the victor not only slept on the battle-ground, but enjoyed the spoils.

But let us leave these men of diminished souls, who give the lie to civilization, and follow the old Indian out into the black and lonely night.

Who can describe the wild torrent that rolled through his soul, as he recoiled and shrunk away from the loathsome tyrant and dastard. The Indian is cruel and merciless in war, but with him as with the Bedouin, the rights of hospitality are sacred. Grey Eagle had always prided himself on this, and had entertained scores of white men who were perfect strangers, without remuneration. To these brutal churls he had, as usual, proffered his all, to which they had retorted with a murderous attack, in his own wigwam. No measure of infamy could equal this. That they could claim his lodge seemed so monstrous a perversion of the eternal principles of justice that he could not understand it. His long-cherished hopes of dying in peace, where his race had lived and died, were blasted in an instant. He thought of the tree at the cave, riven by the lightning stroke, and then the current of his thoughts changed. He thought of his warning, and that the Great Spirit had decreed the events of the day, and taken him from his lodge. At once he prostrated himself in prayer. He then thought of his visitors of the day before. He had formed a high regard for Sydenham and the Doctor, and he longed to see them. He instinctively knew that they were men with the souls of men. They were strangers, but he felt that they would succor and protect him. Mechanically he started towards the river; then he remembered that the raft was on the other side, and that it was to start at midnight. Then he despaired of ever seeing them again. The black night had now shut down and rain began to fall. His fever increased; he could go no farther; his little dog, whining, crouched beside his master.

CHAPTER VIII.

WHILE the infernal discord of evil was being enacted at the bluff, the men on the raft were enjoying an excellent supper, and the cave and the old hermit were the subjects of conversation. All were delighted with the beauty of the cave, and all united in warm commendation of Grey Eagle for his kindness in showing it, &c. Nearly all, too, expressed sympathy for his lonely condition, and utter want of companionship. One of them expressed fears lest he might suffer some harm from lawless hunters; but this idea was scouted at once. As the land would not soon be wanted for cultivation, it was conceded by all that he would not be disturbed, and could end his days in peace, and would secure, by his kind and benevolent acts, the good will of the whites. Indeed, this was known to be the case already, with nearly all the river men.

Soon after supper the men went to bed, but as it was the intention to start at midnight, and as his "watch" began then, Sydenham determined to stay up, and not "spoil the night by a short sleep in the first part of it." Accordingly, he and the Doctor went to their cabin and passed the evening in reading and conversation. At ten o'clock it began to rain, and seeing that it was too dark to float safely, Sydenham retired, and was soon followed by the Doctor.

At daybreak the raft was got under way again, and as

a rise in the river was just coming down, the current was unusually swift.

Just below where the raft had been moored the river bends to the left. It then bends sharply back to the right again, and at the bight of this last bend, the channel sets in close to the Minnesota shore. Here, at a distance from the cave of about one and a half miles, in a direct line, is a broad shelving rock that commands a view of the river below for a long distance. As the raft neared this the raftsmen's ears were saluted with a wild and peculiar sound. It seemed like a human voice, but different from anything they had ever heard. All listened in silence to its wild, mournful wailing. At length one of the men, who had been much among the Indians, said he thought it was the death-song of a Sioux warrior. All eyes were now turned in the direction from which the sound proceeded, but a clump of willows obstructed the view. This was soon passed, and they saw, standing upon the rock, the tall form of Grey Eagle. He was looking down the river, and with his right hand held aloft, was chanting, in the Sioux language, his wild and solemn dirge. At times the measure was slow and plaintive, and then sharp, loud and discordant. As they neared him Sydenham went to the edge of the raft and called to him. He turned toward them, and all were startled at the ghostly and deathlike expression of his face. His dress also was soiled with rain and mud, and spotted with several blood-stains. He did not seem to notice them, but continued the death-song with his face upturned and pointing with his right hand toward the zenith.

"Some accident has happened him," said Sydenham, "or he is mad. Throw her in," he said to the steersman; "we will land and see what is the matter."

The men sprang to obey the order with alacrity; landing was effected a short distance below, and soon the long, even mass grated against the gravelly bank. All landed, but the Doctor suggested that they should not go to him cr attract his attention until his mood changed. Accordingly, they crouched behind the bushes and listened; and this was the death-song of Grey Eagle:

"Great Spirit, God and Father of all men,
And Jesus, Savior of white men and Indians,
Master of all the earth,
Of the clouds and winds, of lightning and thunder,
Of the sun, moon and stars,
Of the white man and Indian,
Of the bear, the elk and buffalo,
Of the little fishes, of the deer,
And of all things;
Oh listen to the voice of the poor Indian,
Grey Eagle is dying, he is passing away,
From the hunting-grounds of his fathers,
His spirit is broken, his heart is gone,
He is too old for war,
He can only die.
The bad white men have come,
When he offered them food and shelter,
They beat and robbed him;
A dog is better than they,
They are worse than a beast.
Destroy them, sweep them away,
For Grey Eagle cannot, he is too old,
He is weak and sick, and will soon die,
His wives and his children are dead,
His kindred are dead
Or gone toward the setting sun.
His tribe have gone,
Hide them from the white men,
Or they will die and be gone.

> Keep them from the bad white men,
> Or much blood will be shed.
> Give power to the good white men,
> Give them children like the leaves of the trees,
> And good deeds like drops of rain.
> Keep away the white men's laws
> From the red men,
> And give to the red men
> Peace and the white men's knowledge.
> And now, Great Spirit and Father,
> Forgive all Indians and all white men,
> Reach out your hand and take Grey Eagle home."

The wild chant ceased, and the raftsmen saw the chief prostrate himself upon the cold rock. Sydenham and the Doctor knew that he was engaged in prayer, and motioned the men to remain quiet. Soon they saw him rise to a sitting posture, and turn his face down the river. Motioning to the men not to show themselves, the two friends walked forward to the rock. The Indian saw them, but gazed vacantly upon them, without any sign of recognition. "Grey Eagle," said Sydenham kindly, "what has happened? what is the matter?" They drew near to him and each gently took one of his hands in theirs. The wildness in his eyes changed, he uttered no word, but his breast heaved and his whole frame trembled with emotion. Tears rolled down his shrunken and emaciated cheeks. Oh! the might, the power, of human kindness and sympathy. This stoic of the woods had borne wounds and torture without a murmur, calamity of all kinds without a tear; but the kind, sympathetic words of the white stranger, went at once to his heart. He told them the story of his wrongs. The Doctor felt his pulse, and found it indicating an alarmed state; he was in a raging fever.

"God is good," said the old chief. "He has sent the

'Young Elk' and his friend to see that Grey Eagle shall not die like a dog and be eaten by wolves."

The men gathered around; the suffering man grasped the hand of each. They took him on board the raft and laid him in Sydenham's bunk. The poor little lame dog followed, and was fed abundantly by the men, and an old coat spread for him to sleep on,—he was adopted by the raftsmen at once.

The Doctor prepared some medicine; but the sick man said, " No use, no use." The Doctor finally prevailed upon him to take something to allay the fever. He then mentioned the name of his old friend, the missionary at St. Paul; and Sydenham told him he would write a letter to him, and send up by the first boat. This done, Sydenham started with the men for Grey Eagle's lodge, leaving two men on the raft with directions to hail the first passing steamboat bound up, and put the letter on board by going out in the skiff.

The Doctor remained with his patient, who seemed in great pain, and was occasionally delirious. The raftsmen took with them their guns. The little dog started to go with them. He then ran back to his old master, whined, and looked wistfully up at the bunk where he lay. He then looked up at the Doctor, who sat beside the bunk, and knew he was a friend. Then he started as fast as he could go, after the party going to his master's old camp, whose errand he seemed to know.

The raftsmen proposed nothing else than to "clean out" the invading robbers. As for Sydenham, he was greatly exasperated, but not at all disposed to take the least advantage on account of the strength of his party. He felt, however, anxious that they should attempt to treat him as they had the poor, helpless Indian. He hoped for this, and felt half inclined to make a special effort to have them do so.

He finally concluded to send on a scout to reconnoitre. Calling "Sandy" to his side, he explained to him that he wanted him to know who and what the party at the lodge were, and that he wanted to know whether or not the fault was wholly on one side before he reached there, especially as the men were excited, and the facts might be learned by one man better than by a display of force.

The intelligent fellow at once expressed his readiness to go on and see what they had to say for themselves, before they knew that any one was in the neighborhood who cared for an Indian's life or rights, and departed with an admonition from Sydenham to keep cool, and not to come back, but stay at the lodge until the party came up. Sandy hurried along at a rapid pace, while the rest went slowly, and finally sat down, and all took a smoke. And this smoke seemed to dispose them all to act with deliberation, and direct their efforts, as Sydenham had indicated, to get at the facts of the whole affair.

When Sandy reached the lodge, they (Brown's party) had not left it, but had just breakfasted, and were preparing to begin the work of surveying—running lines, finding corners, etc. Brown had bought half a section, he said, and wished to have the lines established, and permanent marks placed at each corner. The surveyor said he knew of one "original corner" in the vicinity, established by the United States survey, and proposed to go to that and make it a starting-point.

As Sandy drew near, he recognized Bill Smith, with whom he had once been on a raft, and a colloquy ensued in which all took a part; and Brown, supposing from Sandy's comments, that he was highly gratified at what had been done to the owner of the lodge, made no disguise, but seemed to take some pride in having been the aggressor; and gave a pretty true account of the whole affair, save in the matter of the Indian's trying to rescue his dog; this he persisted in rendering, "The old villain undertook to help his dog against me." At this Bill Smith only grinned, and glared at the huge feet encased in heavy cow-hide boots, and the stalwart form of the speaker.

"Ain't you afraid," said Sandy, "that he will shoot some of you, or get a crowd of red-skins and attack you while you are here; or, after you settle here, if you do settle, that they will retaliate in some way?"

Brown gave an uneasy look, at this, and said he "wished all the d——d Indians were killed or moved a thousand miles farther west." "There are none about here," he said, "except the old squatter who lived here."

"Yes there are," said Sandy; "there are six families and eight men camped ten miles back of here."

Brown started as though a mine had opened, and both Smith and the surveyor looked alarmed.

"Are you sure of this, and how do you know?" they anxiously enquired.

"I was told so yesterday by a man who knows," said Sandy. And so he had been, for when coming down from the cave the day before, he had asked Grey Eagle if there were any other Indians near, and he had mentioned these, as also some on the river.

Smith reflected. He knew the vengeful Indian character, and supposed Grey Eagle like all the rest. He knew full well the heinousness of the outrage done him, and that he had gone at once to the Indian camp he had no doubt, not knowing that in his feeble state this was impossible.

He thought of his own exposed life, hunting through the woods alone, and how easy it would be for an Indian to shoot him from behind a tree. Brown lived in Wisconsin, and could stay there, if necessary, and the surveyor too would be safe enough; he alone would have to suffer for it all. As for getting possession of the coveted rifle, this he now saw would be the height of folly, and sure to get him into trouble. As he thought of all this, he felt a fierce rage against Brown, whom he thought was the cause of it all. He was at once greatly frightened and enraged. While in this state of mind he saw a party of men approaching. It was Sydenham and the raftsmen. Relieved to see that they were white men, and not Indians, as he had at first glance thought they might be, he went out to meet them. Sydenham he knew, having once been saved by him from drowning, when he had got drunk and fallen off a raft. He was overjoyed to see him, and very hearty and demonstrative, but his reception by Sydenham and all the men was chilling. Brown and the surveyor also felt sure of their scalps for the present, and safe against the eight Indian warriors, when they saw the rifles and stalwart forms of the raftsmen.

Sydenham did not bid good morning, or ask an invitation to enter. Sandy had whispered a few words in his ear, and he knew Brown and his guilt.

That worthy was sitting upon Grey Eagle's bed of skins beside the surveyor, examining a plat of the township, which was spread upon their knees. He was a little surprised that the party entered without his invitation, but supposed it was by the invitation of Bill Smith. That individual, however, was outside, having a word with Sandy.

"Glad to see you, gentlemen," said Brown, "glad to

see you, for we had just heard news that made us feel a little uneasy, lest some of you should be killed and scalped by some d——d Indians they say are hanging around, a few miles back."

"Ah," said Sydenham, "why should you be afraid? The Indians are peaceable, and the hunters and fur-buyers say they can go anywhere among them with bags of silver coin, and be safer than among white men, if known to have money. 'The word of a Sioux is good.'"

We have said that Brown was a self-sufficient, overbearing man, always determined to have his own way, and inclined to play the bully.

The words of Sydenham were calmly spoken, but his eye blazed with a stern accusation that somewhat awed and yet angered him.

"The reason I thought there was danger from them just now," he said, "was that we had a difficulty with an old Indian squatter, in the course of which I knocked him down; and he went away to bring the others down on us."

"Ah," said Sydenham, "where did you have the fracas."

"Oh, right here," said Brown, "here in the wigwam."

He then went on to give an account of the affair, much more favorable to himself than that given to Sandy; yet the essential facts, though obscured, still remained. Sydenham heard him through patiently and then spoke:

"You came to this poor old man's lodge and assaulted and maimed his dog for merely barking to give warning of your approach. You then entered the lodge rudely, but yet the Indian, instead of compelling you to leave, tendered you his hospitality. You replied with a menace; and then the little dog attacked but could not possibly hurt you. You attempted to mangle or kill the dog—which you had already wantonly injured—right under his master's roof and before his face. He, it seems, tried to save his faithful dog from your brutal violence, without hurting you; and then you struck him to the earth, and afterwards dragged his insensible body out of his own lodge, which you have since occupied. No wonder you are afraid of vengeance from Indians! It is such villains as you that bring on trouble, and jeopardize the lives of hundreds of helpless families on the frontier; and for this, as well as for the wrong done to the Indian, you shall be punished. You shall not play the ruffian and robber with impunity. There is law enough to reach you; and it shall be enforced."

Brown was thunderstruck, amazed, frightened. He felt somewhat as a country village bully on his first visit to the city might feel in finding himself in the grasp of the police. As Sydenham spoke in a firm (and somewhat loud and angry) tone, his face alternately flushed with rage and paled with fear. He looked around, and saw only the stern and angry looks of resolute men bent on him. He turned to the surveyor by his side, but that gentleman saw clearly that the wind of popular sentiment had changed during the night, and blew now rather strong from another quarter; and he had no notion of opposing it. If in favor of Brown, he prepared to drift until he should get in a crowd where that side would be strongest. But he had fears that that would not happen, and so gave him no sympathy or support.

Brown glared around him like a wolf caught in a trap. He called out for Bill Smith, but that individual made no response. He had heard of the summary practice of lynch law; and he thought the crowd had come to lynch him. His face became livid, and he quivered in every limb with fear and rage. At length he spoke out that "it was his land; he had bought it and paid for it, and no one had any business on it without his leave.

Among Sydenham's crew there was a large-framed, powerful and good-natured man named James Brady. He was a very quiet and peaceable man, but, when once roused to anger, he was like a roused lion. He had felt great indignation at the treatment of Grey Eagle, and now that the whole matter was proven, this was intensified. But the last assertion of Brown was the straw too much; it was the spark that fired the magazine of his wrath.

"You d——d scoundrel," he said in a voice of thunder; "do you tell me I have no right to walk through these wild woods without your leave?" and as he spoke he doubled his fist and raised his arm in a menacing manner.

Brown saw that his peculiar ideas of the rights of ownership were not "healthy" in that locality; and he replied, slowly and deprecatingly:

"You have no right to cut my timber without my consent."

"Timber be d——d," said the raftsman, "who is talking of cutting timber? You come here talking this d——d meanness, and, like a d——d coward, almost murder a helpless old Indian; and now, when a man faces you who is able to thrash the devil out of you, you talk about cutting timber."

"Has not a man a right to forbid another to come on to his premises?" said Brown, appealing to the surveyor.

Thus appealed to, Farley deliberated with great gravity for a moment or two, and then replied:

"If a man has his land fenced, he may forbid another to come inside his enclosure by proper notice."

"You," said Sydenham, "are a stranger here; and who knows your ownership or the boundaries of your land?"

"I have here a certificate of entry," said Brown, "from the Land Office at St. Paul;" and he handed the paper to Sydenham, who looked at it and made a careful memorandum in his pocket-book of Brown's name.

"This is your name is it?" he said, turning to Brown.

That brave man had partly recovered from his fear of being lynched by the raftsmen; but this question awakened another fear—that of being arrested and punished by law, and he hesitated about answering, lest a warrant should be issued for him; but finally concluded that it would be useless for him to deny his name, and so answered that it was.

This hesitation, however, had been noticed by all the men; and Brady, whose wrath had not cooled, at once challenged Brown to a fist-fight. This invitation Brown very mildly declined; and Sydenham, fearing Brady would assault him, took Brady one side and explained his intention to have Brown arrested, and, if possible, punished legally; and requested Brady to let him alone, which he promised to do.

He then told the men that Grey Eagle had wanted them to bring all his things to the raft. Accordingly, the men stripped the covering from the lodge-poles, folded it carefully, collected all the various articles that belonged to the chief, and, dividing the weight among them, started for the raft. Sydenham took the surveyor one side, and explained to him the necessity of righting this wrong in a proper way, and the deep interest the people of the neighborhood had in seeing to it that it was done. Farley did not say much, but, after considerable urging, he gave Sydenham his word that he would make no effort to avoid being subpenaed as a witness, and that he would not throw any obstacle in the way of a fair and speedy trial.

This settled, Sydenham called Bill Smith; and they walked out some distance on the way towards the raft. Pausing then, Sydenham spoke:

"Bill, did I not save your life once?"

"Yes, Captain, you did; and I will never forget it," said the hunter.

"Well, Bill," said Sydenham, "I now wish to ask you to act like a man about this affair."

"How, Captain? what do you mean?" inquired Bill.

"Why, simply this: You, I know, are an Indian-hater, and think a wrong done to an Indian is simply no wrong at all."

"That's a good deal so, Captain; yet I felt sorry for the old man when this big fellow abused him."

"Well, Bill, I want you to promise me three or four things. One is that you will drink no whisky before Wednesday."

"That's a long time, Cap.; but I'll promise you not to drink but a small swig before breakfast."

"All right," said Sydenham; "now promise me that you will not talk with Brown about this Indian affair."

"I promise," said Bill.

"Now promise to be on hand at the trial, and tell the whole and exact truth."

"I will," said Smith, "and here's my hand on it."

They shook hands and Sydenham followed on to the raft, while Bill went back to carry chain.

CHAPTER IX.

ON arrival at the raft Sydenham selected a suitable spot on the river bank, and directed the men to cut lodge-poles, and set up the lodge just as it had been, and place the articles belonging to Grey Eagle inside. He then went on board the raft and found the chief asleep.

A steamer had just passed up the river, and the letter had been sent to the missionary at St. Paul.

Telling the Doctor what had passed, Sydenham, then, accompanied by Sandy, started for the little town six miles below. Arrived there, he went to the Justice of the Peace, and soon succeeded in having the constable dispatched on horseback with a warrant for Brown, and subpœnas for Bill Smith and Farley as witnesses. The Justice showed little disposition to act at first, in a case of an Indian against a white man, yet he finally agreed with Sydenham, that justice demanded, and the public interest required, that an examination should be had. After getting some refreshment, the two then started back, the hour of the trial having been fixed at nine o'clock the following morning.

The constable succeeded in effecting the arrest of Brown, and served the subpœnas upon the necessary witnesses; and, as the above hour approached, the vicinity of the magistrate's office was thronged by a mixed gathering of men, boys, a few Indians and a few squaws.

At the time of which we write, there were more or less of the original Indian population scattered over the whole of Minnesota, though some bands had drawn back to the extreme western and unsettled parts. This was the case with that branch of the great Sioux nation to which Grey Eagle belonged. The whites, therefore, were the more disposed to avoid difficulties with the Indians that might lead to serious results. And so, on the occasion of this trial, although with many the prejudices against the Indians were strong, yet Grey Eagle had, through the official action of Sydenham and the support of the raftsmen, almost an even chance for that public sympathy which so often influences the course of justice. Sydenham had engaged a lawyer (at his own expense) with whom he was acquainted, to prosecute Brown, who had also found a lawyer to defend him. To give all the details of the trial, the arguments of the lawyers, the evidence of the witnesses, etc., etc., would occupy more space than we care to devote to that use. Briefly then: the jury was impaneled, and the witnesses examined, re-examined and cross-questioned, according to the most approved usage in such cases, the jury of course cudgeling their brains, as usual, to sift the few facts from the vast amount of verbiage.

Bill Smith, of course, was the principal witness, and upon his testimony, undoubtedly, the case hinged. And right fortunate was it that he had been forewarned by Sydenham, and a promise exacted from him, to hold no conversation with Brown upon the subject, and to avoid whisky. That worthy had tried to prepare the mind of Smith to testify that he struck the Indian in self-defence; but Smith invariably began a long hunting yarn, and left no chance. Brown finally hinted at a handsome present of money, but Smith only continued on another branch of his hunting adventures. He tried whisky, thinking to thus deaden his sensibilities; but Bill remembered his promise to Sydenham—the man who had saved his life— and excused himself on the ground of a headache. And so it came to pass that when he was put upon the witness stand, he complied fully with his oath, and told the truth without bent or bias, and all the examination and cross-questioning of the defence only made it clearer. Brown was allowed to tell his own story; but when the whole testimony of all the witnesses was concluded, it only made his case the worse. The little dog was brought into court by a ragged Indian, who pointed to Brown's huge boots and burly form, and then to the little beast, with a grimace that greatly amused the crowd, and annoyed Brown and his lawyer. Finally the case was given to the jury, and, after a short absence, they brought in a verdict of *Guilty*, and Brown was sentenced to pay a fine of fifty dollars and costs.

This verdict gave great satisfaction to a majority of the assemblage, and, paltry as was the punishment, Sydenham had expected no more.

The charge had been made of unprovoked assault and battery. This, the lawyer had advised him, would be pretty sure to be sustained; whereas, as Grey Eagle's outward physical injuries were slight, graver charges might not be, and he might be acquitted. The deep, deadly and murderous wounds to the high spirit of the old chief, the law provided no remedy for.

The news of the trial had spread, and quite a number of Indians had assembled, and were intermingled with the whites in the crowd in and about the little court-room. The tall forms of these Sioux (for the men would average very nearly six feet in height, and they were powerfully built) were quite conspicuous in the crowd. There were also some squaws: these were jubilant when the result of the trial was made known. The men were stoical and grave, as usual, but their eyes expressed satisfaction. They were soon shaking hands with the whites. One old chief approached the magistrate with grave courtesy and dignity, and shook hands with him. He then went through the same ceremony with the prosecuting attorney, jurors and witnesses, and all this without speaking a word. When he came to Bill Smith, he said, " You hate Indians, but you tell truth this time." This provoked a smile from many who knew the hunter, and that to testify truly for an Indian against a white man must have cost him a great effort. Unusual good-will seemed to exist between the two dissimilar races. Upon the whole, it was a pleasant scene; justice had been appeased, and peace followed in her train.

The trial ended, Sydenham did not wait for the friendly greetings of the Indians, but gathered his men, paid his lawyer, and started for the raft. The day was almost spent, and the sun was getting low, when he reached the raft. Altogether, the time lost would have sufficed to float his raft more than a hundred miles down the river; and he was anxious to make a speedy passage. An Indian runner had preceded him, and carried the news of the result. The Doctor was indignant that the punishment was so trivial, but made no comment.

Grey Eagle lay in a tranquil state in the bunk, where he had been placed. The medicines had produced the desired effect, and the fever had abated, but had left the vital powers at so low an ebb that his recovery was doubtful, the Doctor thought. As Sydenham approached the bunk, the Indian extended his hand and grasped that of the white man.

"The Young Elk's heart is big, and his hand is strong. He is just and wise. May he live long, and serve the Great Spirit by just deeds between the white and red men; for both are often bad, and the spirit of evil has great power over them. Has the Young Elk a wife?"

Sydenham replied that he had not.

"Has he father and mother, brothers and sisters?"

Sydenham replied that he had not; that all were dead.

The old chief did not speak for some minutes; at length he said:

"Grey Eagle has lived alone, and would have died alone like a dog, had it not been for the Young Elk; but the young should mate. Has the Young Elk no maiden whom he loves?"

"No," said Sydenham, wonderingly, and yet interested. "I have none. I have lived much in the woods where there were none to be seen."

The old chief lay silent for some time, with one hand over his face, and the other clasping Sydenham's. At length he spoke as though dreaming:

"I see the young white chief at Grey Eagle's cave; beside him is a young white woman, beautiful as the stars at night. She has come out of a cloud that was like fire, to his arms, and is his wife. He shows her the inner cave, and talks to her of Grey Eagle, and she weeps. Dark clouds cover them, but the sunshine of love warms them, and the Great Spirit shields them from evil. Sons and daughters are born, and their house is built upon a rock, and the red man is not forgotten."

Grey Eagle uttered these words in a dreamy tone, his voice seeming to have diminished to almost a whisper.

The Doctor felt his pulse and found it excited. Sydenham withdrew, and motioned to the men to avoid all noise near the little cabin, where the sick man lay.

It was now dark, and lights were placed on each outside corner of the raft. The boat from St. Paul was now hourly expected, with the missionary on board. A few Indians had come up to see the old chief; and these built a fire on shore, and occupied the lodge that had been set up there. About nine o'clock in the evening, the expected steamer arrived, and opposite the raft, stopped her engines, and the captain hailed the raft, enquiring whether that was the place where Father Martel was expected. Upon receiving the answer that it was, the yawl was lowered, manned by two men, a passenger entered, and the yawl was sculled rapidly to the raft.

Sydenham and the Doctor received the good missionary. He was an old man of a mild and benevolent countenance, but one that indicated energy and mental activity. His manner was very grave, yet kindly After some little conversation in regard to Grey Eagle's condition, etc., Sydenham led the way to his bedside. The Indian had heard the steamer, the voice of the captain, and the approach of the yawl; and when Father Martel approached his bedside, he expressed his gratitude in a voice husky with emotion. The raftsmen and the Indians from the shore gathered around, while by the light of the torch the solemn service of the Catholic church was performed. After it was over, the chief signified his wish to be alone, and all save the missionary withdrew; and we must now return to some of the other personages of our story.

CHAPTER X.

AFTER the trial was over, we have said the result was very satisfactory to the assembled crowd. We should, however, qualify this by saying a *majority* of the assembled crowd. It was in this something like the result of an election, highly satisfactory to the successful candidates and dominant party, but a matter disagreeable and even disgusting to the defeated candidates and the minority party.

Brown was gloomy and taciturn. Had he been sentenced to solitary confinement for a time, he would have had abundant opportunity for reflection, and conscience and self-crimination would have had a healthy effect upon him, and he would have come out a better man, or at least a less troublesome and vicious man. As it was, he was mulcted in a sum for fine and costs that he did not greatly feel,—only that money, being a thing he sincerely loved, the loss of it caused some considerable grief.

Bill Smith he now hated bitterly, and dismissed at once from his service, and engaged a village idler who professed warm sympathy for him and hatred of "white Indians," to carry chain in his place.

After the departure of the raftsmen and Indians, the "majority" seemed to be on the side of Brown; and the surveyor, who had very little to testify to as a witness, but been quietly scenting for the true course that "public opinion" would take, now found voice and tongue, and, curiously enough, "popped up" right alongside of Brown. There is a species of small, wild ducks, known to sportsmen as "Dippers," who, before percussion caps came into use, would, it is said, dive at the flash of the gun, and after remaining under water a considerable time, would come up in a place where they were least expected. Farley had found it necessary to dive for a time, but had now popped up alongside of Brown, at the little village tavern, where a thirsty crowd had gathered expecting that *somebody* would treat.

Sydenham had gone off and left this great duty unperformed. In this he had not shown good Generalship—left his rear open to attack.

Brown walked doggedly into the bar-room and began grumbling and scolding abont the result. The jurymen did not happen to be about. He soon found two or three supporters, and the case was argued over, and very naturally, in this informal appeal, but one side was argued. As the case was now viewed, Brown was on his own land, and had some provocation from the dog; and when he struck the old man he said he did not mean to hurt him, and it was contended that he was not hurt, and that his present sickness might not have anything to do with it. Indeed it was said that he was often sick and unable to leave his lodge. At this stage Brown called for the drinks for all hands, and nearly all drank. After this the general verdict was, that after all, Brown was not a bad fellow, and that upon the whole, he was rather an aggrieved and injured man. Some even said he had only served the Indian right; but Grey Eagle was so well known and liked that this atrocious sentiment found but little favor.

Brown was in great haste to finish his survey, and start for home, and soon called for his team, and, accompanied by the surveyor and the new chain-bearer, started up the river,—not, however, till he had privately counseled with the landlord as to whether he would be in danger from the Indians. He was assured that he need have no apprehensions; that the Indians had attended the trial, had been satisfied with the result, and that the chief and others had shaken hands, and had pledged their word to the Justice that Brown should not be hurt.

"Now," said the landlord, "you are safe, perfectly so, from these Indians, and so ought to be satisfied with the trial; for, had it not been for that, your life would not have been safe."

He was an old Indian trader, and his word was considered the best authority in the neighborhood; and, although he kept the house where this one-sided discussion had been held, he had not expressed one word of sympathy for Brown. On the contrary, he thought his punishment wholly inadequate.

Brown drove rapidly out of town and up the river. Arrived at his land, the work of surveying was entered upon at once. As this work progressed, he felt considerable dissatisfaction, and regretted that he had not gone out on the smooth prairies, back from the river, where, the surveyor told him, there was still some good land not yet "entered;" good soil, free from rocks, stumps and bluffs. Here, a large share of his land would be the steep bluff sides, useless for cultivation, while the remainder was mostly covered with a forest, the timber of which, although of some value in itself, would be greatly in the way in getting the land under cultivation, and involve a heavy expense for clearing. It was even worse than he had expected, from what he had seen, the day of his arrival.

This, and the result of the trial, the fine, etc., made the man very gloomy and ill-natured.

CHAPTER XI.

WE left Grey Eagle alone with Father Martel. To him he confided the disposition of his little property, which he knew had been rescued by Sydenham from the clutches of Brown and his party. His rifle and hunting equipments he wished to give Sydenham; his lodge of skins to the good Father himself, to use in any way he thought fit. The skins that constituted his bedding, etc., he gave, part to the Doctor; and the remainder he wished divided among the men. Various other small articles he wished divided among such of the Indians as came to his burial: for, although the Doctor had not despaired of his recovery, yet the old warrior felt that he was dying. After the allotment of these presents, Grey Eagle paused for some moments; he then spoke:

"Good Father, you white men say that old men become childish. Perhaps Grey Eagle is so now, for he longs to have his body buried near the little waterfall, at the head of the little valley in which his lodge stood; for there lie many of his blood. Promise me, good Father, that this shall be so."

"I promise you that it shall be as you wish," said Father Martel.

The chief then expressed his readiness to die, and his joy and gratitude to God for the promise of everlasting life in a future world, and for death among friends. He then desired the presence of Sydenham and the Doctor, both of whom entered the cabin and took seats by his side.

The Doctor soon saw that a change was taking place, and that death was near. The chief grasped their hands and attempted to speak, but could not. At the invitation of the missionary, those of the men who were up entered the cabin and gathered around the bunk. The dying man gave each a look of recognition, but did not move or speak. A few minutes more passed in silence, and the Doctor placed his hand upon his pulse. It had ceased to beat. The soul of Grey Eagle had passed away.

The morning came, and preparations were made for the burial. The Indians on the shore sent a runner to others, and soon quite a number had assembled, and their plaintive wailing was heard during the entire forenoon.

Meantime, Sydenham, accompanied by the missionary, with two of his men bearing shovels, had gone to dig the grave. They both had misgivings that if the spot indicated by Grey Eagle should chance to be on the land entered by Brown, that that noble lord of the soil might object. Yet, both had almost felt ashamed that they had harbored a suspicion of this kind. Neither of these men had learned that a thoroughly evil heart is a spring from which evil issues continually. The fall was soon reached, and, in a sheltered nook of the little valley, enclosed on the side next the bluff by a semi-circular wall of almost perpendicular rocks, and close to the waterfall, but on dry and suitable ground, they found the indications of a number of Indian graves. Father Martel selected a spot near the middle of the burying place, and shaded by a large elm tree. The men marked out a grave and began digging. After a time, Sydenham and the missionary took the shovels and worked while the others rested. In this way they relieved each other, and, in a little while, the grave was finished. As they were about leaving, to meet the funeral cortege, they saw a party coming down the hill, just above the cascade. It was Brown and the surveying party. they ran the line, and it passed a few rods *above* the fall; so Brown owned all the valley, including the cascade and the Indian burial-place. The surveying party did not see the grave-diggers until they had crossed the ravine and began ascending the hill. The chain-bearer then saw them, and called to Brown:

"There's a lot of them fellers down in the holler digging."

Brown stopped and looked; and it flashed upon him that Grey Eagle was dead, and they were digging his grave. For a moment a twinge of remorse shot through his small, tough, hard conscience. This element, however, did not predominate in his character; and its momentary ascendancy was soon lost. The next emotion was fear. He felt fearful of another arrest, and of more serious consequences, and reflected upon it for some minutes. Finally, he concluded in his own mind that they couldn't make anything on the ground of causing the Indian's death, as he had got up and walked away, and they had reported him sick with fever. Besides, by law, a man could not be tried twice for the same offense. He sent Holmes, the chain-bearer, to see "what was up." On his return with the news of the Indian's death, as no mention was made of him, he felt bolder

"D——n them!" he said; "they have no business making a graveyard of my land; and I have a mind to warn them off."

"I would," said Holmes.

The surveyor now came up; and Brown appealed to him.

"You have a right to prohibit their burying on your land, when you can clearly show that it is yours," said that cautious individual.

"Well," said Brown, "can't you testify that it is on my land?"

"It certainly is on the land as numbered in your certificate."

"Well, then," said Brown, "I can prove by you that it is my land."

Accordingly the trio started for the grave, where Sydenham and his party were awaiting the approach of the funeral cortege, which was to start from the raft under the direction of the Doctor.

"Did you know that this hole you have dug was on my land?" said Brown, addressing Sydenham.

"No; I did not," said Sydenham.

"Well, it is," said Brown, "as Mr. Farley, here, the surveyor, can tell you."

"Yes," said Farley, "the line runs about where that oak tree stands,"—pointing, at the same time, to a tree, about fifty yards above the falls.

Just then the funeral procession appeared in sight, at the distance of about two hundred yards. The corpse was enclosed in a rude coffin, made by the men of boards from the raft, and was borne upon the shoulders of four stalwart Sioux Indians. Behind it walked the Doctor, with most of the men from the raft, a number of Indian men, a few squaws and some children. The procession was grave and orderly, the only sound heard being the lamentations of the squaws. Arrived at the grave, the rude bier was placed upon the ground; and both Indians and white men gazed with wonder and indignation upon Brown.

"Well," said Sydenham, who had been musing for some minutes, "suppose the land is yours; what of it?"

"Why," said Brown, doggedly, "I don't want it used for a graveyard; that is all."

A fierce, angry murmur ran through the assembled crowd, from both white men and Indians: a word or sign from Sydenham, and terrible vengeance would have been wreaked upon the spot.

"Men," said Sydenham, turning to the crowd, "we have come here to bury the dead. We must have no violence or angry quarrel with this man."

Motioning, then, to the Doctor, the missionary and one or two chiefs, he led them to one side to discuss what should be done.

Among the Indians there was a wild, hare-brained and supposed to be half-idiotic fellow, named by the whites "Joe," and looked upon by his own tribe as but half-witted. Joe had watched all the proceedings with intense interest, his eyes almost starting from their sockets. Joe, when he saw the consultation going on at a little distance, left the crowd and approached Sydenham, in a high state of excitement, and thus addressed him:

"Don't bury Grey Eagle on that bad white man's land, or he will dig him up and give his body to the wolves and steal his blanket. I know it," said Joe, "for I saw white men, away down the river, throw dead Indian out of tree and steal blanket and bear-skins. Don't do it," said Joe; "bury him somewhere else where they can't find him."

The poor fellow gesticulated wildly, and seemed greatly excited. He was told they would bury Grey Eagle safely, and that he should not be disturbed. The chiefs then directed him to go back.

After some consultation it was determined to make an effort to purchase the ground necessary for a grave, if possible, but in no case to have any further difficulty with Brown, but to get away from his revolting presence as soon as possible.

Accordingly the party returned to the grave; and Rev. Father Martel spoke, addressing Brown:

"This man, whose remains we come here to bury, not knowing that this was your land, or that you would object, if it was requested me to see that he was buried on this spot. It was his dying wish, and I promised on his dying bed that it should be done; now we are here, and his grave is dug; we ask if you will not sell us ground enough on which to bury him."

Brown now spoke to the surveyor, and the two walked to one side. While they were gone, poor Joe, wild with excitement, mounted upon a fragment of rock and harangued the crowd:

"Don't, I tell you, bury Grey Eagle on bad man's land. He will dig him up; wolves will eat him; evil spirits will take away his bones, and Grey Eagle will never enter the happy hunting ground." Here, throwing his arms wildly up, he went on: "Joe lay in bushes away down big river, and saw white men throw dead Indian down out of big tree, and take away rifle, powder, tomahawk, bear-skins and blanket, leaving Indian body naked and broken on the ground."

At this a wild wail rose from the squaws, and the warriors knit their brows, and their eyes blazed with a frenzy of rage; but, controlled by the missionary and Sydenham, they stood silent and motionless.

Brown came back and said to Sydenham: "I won't sell a small piece of the land, or have it used; but I will sell it all to you; and you can do what you please with it."

Here there was a pause; finally the missionary called Sydenham and the Doctor to one side, and urged them to buy it, if Brown would sell it for a fair price; if not, he saw no other alternative but to go elsewhere for a grave.

After a few words of consultation, the friends concluded that the first thing would be to enquire the price.

Brown, when interrogated upon this point, said if they would pay him back the price he paid at the land office, (one dollar and a quarter per acre), and give him one hundred dollars, they should have the land. This would make in all five hundred dollars for the half-section.

Again the friends consulted. Neither of them had cared to buy land in that locality, nor had either money enough with him for that purpose. The Doctor thought he could not command any means, short of St. Louis, unless by chance he could borrow from some friend in St. Paul. Sydenham had no more money with him than would suffice for his use, but had enough in the bank at St. Paul to pay for the land. Finally it was agreed that Sydenham should buy and retain the land, using therefor the ready money that both had with them, and should send to St. Paul for his money to be forwarded at once to Wenona, or some point below.

Sydenham then signified his acceptance of Brown's proposition, on condition that Farley should finish the survey, and establish the lines and corners, at Brown's expense, and then come at once down to the neighboring town and execute the necessary papers, to be prepared by Sydenham's lawyer, and receive the money. Brown placed his certificate of entry in Farley's hands, and Sydenhan deposited with the same party, twenty-five dollars; the white men present being called upon to witness the agreement.. The whole matter was explained to the Indians; but they were not satisfied. They thoroughly distrusted Brown, and feared treachery unless the writing on paper was done at once. Finally the chief signified to Brown to leave the money and paper in the missionary's hands, which he consented to do, greatly to the satisfaction of the Indians, and of some of the whites who had no confidence in the surveyor. Brown consented to the change quite gracefully. His feelings had at length reacted; he had, as he thought, made a good trade, and he felt (for him) quite genial and kind. The presence of the dead body of the man whose days he had shortened by violence had but little effect.

To Sydenham and the Doctor, Brown's presence was intolerable; and it was stipulated that not a moment's time should be lost in completing the survey; that the surveying party should proceed with the work at once. To this no objection was made; and Sydenham and his friends felt a sense of relief as though rid of a nightmare of evil, when the burly form of Brown and his party disappeared in the bushes.

The priest now proceeded with the funeral ceremonies, according to the forms of the Roman Catholic Church. White men and Indians listened reverently, with bowed and uncovered heads. The body was lowered into the grave, and it was filled up and a mound raised over it, after the manner of white men. The Indians then brought large stones, as large as they could carry, from the foot of the cascade, and covered this mound completely. The raftsmen brought also a large slab, and set upright at the head of the grave, and a smaller one at the foot. Powder was then sprinkled upon the grave, among the stones, and on the ground near; both white men and Indians believing this would keep wolves and other wild animals away.

When all was done, the Indian men, followed by the squaws and children, formed a procession and marched slowly around the grave singing a wild dirge in the Sioux language. This lasted some time. When it was over Father Martel dismissed the assemblage with a benediction. And so the body of the Indian, Grey Eagle, found decent burial at the hands of men who recognized the rights of humanity and its obligations and duties. Not a man, white or red, left the ground but was morally and spiritually bettered by this triumph of humanity, and human sympathy, over baseness and brutality. The very stars shed a sweeter light into the little dell that night than if Brown had had his unopposed will and way. The raft had been delayed three days; but a great wrong had been righted as far as it could be, and a greater one prevented. The old chief had been assaulted in his own home; but he had not been allowed to perish miserably and unaided. He had been most kindly cared for in his sickness, and the services of religion and of friendship had surrounded his death-bed, and an honored christian burial had been given him, and his grave was safe on the spot where he had so long wished it should be. Moreover, a collision between the whites and Indians, with all its horrors, had been prevented, and, in spite of the death of Grey Eagle, and the baseness of Brown, more confidence and friendly feeling than previously existed had been established.

Such were the reflections of Sydenham, as he walked through the woods toward the raft, whither most of the party had preceded him. The great loss of time, and consequent expense, was, to him, a serious matter; but he felt that he had done his duty, and was well repaid. As to the land, he knew that he could enter plenty that was more valuable at the government price, yet the wild, romantic scenery of the place pleased him. Then he thought of the cave; and the words of the dying chief shot like lightning through his mind: "I see the young white chief at Grey Eagle's cave; beside him is a young white woman beautiful as the stars. She has come out of a cloud that was like fire, to his arms, and is his wife. He paused and sat down upon a log. At the time, he had taken but little notice of the words of the sick man in his delirium; but now every fibre of his frame thrilled with emotion, and his mind embraced it at once, as the electic current passes over the conducting wires.

> "There are moments, I think, when the spirit receives
> Whole volumes of thought on its unwritten leaves."

He was a man of ardent, impulsive nature, and of deep and powerful feelings. He was of that temperament "over which," Bancroft says, "beauty possesses a wonderful and mysterious power." Though he had often felt this power, and, indeed, never failed to feel it when brought within the circle of its attraction, yet the woman who should be

> "The ocean, to the river of his thoughts,"

he had never met; yet he believed

> "If thou art to have a wife of thy youth,
> She is now living on the earth."

What wonder, then, at his emotion. Any bachelor who would not sometimes be moved by such thoughts must have been born under the influence of some of the outside planets.

CHAPTER XII.

ARRIVED at the river side, Father Martel distributed Grey Eagle's little property as he had directed, and so kindly, justly and gracefully did he discharge this difficult duty that even those who received very little or nothing manifested no dissatisfaction. The good Father left the lodge-covering, given him, in care of an infirm old Indian, who he learned was living in a very poor one, telling him to use it as long as he wished. Sydenham, feeling that the present of the rifle and hunting accoutrements seemed a considerable share of the whole, and knowing how great a luxury wheaten flour is to Indians, distributed a considerable quantity among them, to their great satisfaction. He also gave the squaws and children a present of some sugar, to their great delight. A few urgent appeals for tobacco were also supplied.

Father Martel was going down on the raft as far as the little town; but before it shoved off he called all the Indians together and gave them some good advice, after which he read a short prayer and gave them his benediction. The Indians then shook hands with all the raftsmen, and manifested their good-will in their own peculiar way, toward all, but toward Sydenham in particular.

Bill Smith, whose views had been entirely changed, through the explanations of Sydenham and Father Martel, of all that had seemed to him mysterious and supernatural in Grey Eagle's character and mode of life, and who had not been forgotten in the distribution of presents, was now in a condition of perfect friendship with the Indians, and avowed that he had "learned a heap in the last four days."

Before the raft finally shoved off, the surveying party (who had finished their work) came by in their wagon, on their way to town, and Brown called out that he would meet Sydenham at the tavern. It was now almost dark, and the Indians who would camp there that night had lighted their fires.

Bill Smith expressed a wish to go back to the town, "and see the thing entirely through," and accordingly stayed on the raft. The lines were now cast off, the poles were brought into requisition, and the raft slowly drifted out from shore. The Indians stood ranged along the shore in the firelight, and gave a parting salute as they receded from view.

An hour and a half brought the raft to the little town. With some trouble, a landing was effected, and Sydenham, the Doctor and the missionary, with Smith and one or two of the men, went at once to the lawyer's office. Here they found Brown awaiting them, as also the surveyor, who reported his work completed in proper form, and gave Sydenham a memorandum of survey, boundaries and corners. But in the conveyance of the property by deed, from Brown to Sydenham, a difficulty presented itself, on account of the absence of Brown's wife; she being in Wisconsin. Sydenham was determined not to allow the slightest chance for future trouble with Brown, on account of any willfulness, perversity, or dishonesty, in that individual, and finally his lawyer, Mr. Bently, suggested a plan that was agreed to and adopted. By this, Brown executed a full warranty deed, and also a special bond, that he would have his wife execute and send within one month, her quit-claim deed; Sydenham paying him three hundred dollars down, and leaving two hundred with Mr. Bently, to be paid on receipt of the quit-claim deed executed by Brown's wife. The deed, bond and certificate of entry were delivered to Sydenham, and Mr. Bently also gave him a receipt for the two hundred dollars left in his hands, stating the use to which it was to be applied, a duplicate of which was given to Brown. Sydenham then left the deed (together with recording fees for both deeds), in the hands of Mr. Bently, to have placed upon the public records at the county seat. The business concluded, the party from the raft bade Father Martel good-bye (he intending to wait for the first boat for St. Paul), and started for the raft, accompanied by Mr. Bently. That gentleman took a deep interest in the whole case, and the acquaintance between him and Sydenham, which had been slight, seemed to be rapidly ripening into warm friendship. A gentleman and a man of honor and education, with a strong sense of justice and humanity, he appreciated fully the whole matter, and a strong bond of sympathy, friendship and esteem was at once established between himself, Sydenham and the Doctor. After expressing his warm approval of the course pursued by Sydenham, he told him the property he had been almost compelled to buy—aside from its romantic beauty of scenery and association and historical interest, possessed intrinsic value in the great quantity of wood which could be cut upon it, for which the steamers navigating the river afforded a good market, and that after being partially cleared in this way, it would make a pretty good farm, well adapted to the rearing of sheep. He also promised to look after the property, which, with the assistance

Smith, the hunter, promised, he could easily do. Arrived at the raft the friends bade each other a warm and earnest good-bye. Again the raft was shoved from the shore and drifted away in the starlight night.

The Doctor soon retired to rest; but Sydenham's watch was "on" and he had now time to reflect in silence, in the lonely night, upon the strange events of the past few days.

CHAPTER XIII.

THE morning was clear and pleasant, and a bright May sun was shining upon the raft, when our friends were roused by the call to breakfast.

Of course at the breakfast table the events of the few preceding days were discussed, and the raftsmen expressed their opinion of Brown in terms more vigorous than polite. Sydenham felt, however, such a sense of relief in getting rid of him and his evil deeds, that he almost felt disposed to overlook all that he had done. The long delay caused him to feel more impatient of the slightest delay henceforward, as it was of the highest importance to him, in a business sense, to market his lumber as soon as possible, and return without delay to St. Paul.

As yet, the voyage was not much more than well begun; and, while delayed in righting wrongs that happened to lie in his path, a great number of rafts had passed him, some of which were destined for a market as far south as he proposed to go, and he had the rather unpleasant reflection, to him, that the advantage of being first in market, he had lost. However, he said but little, but gave strict attention to the management of the raft, telling the men that for little articles that were occasionally wanted, they must row ahead in the skiff and get them at the towns they were passing, as he did not intend to land the raft except when absolutely unavoidable.

During the forenoon, the Doctor, seeing his friend take

up with business, and engrossed in his own thoughts, was obliged to betake himself to his books. In the afternoon, however, the weather was so delightful, and the raft making such fine progress, the two soon found themselves together, watching the beautiful shores and the lofty bluffs. The Doctor seemed lost in a reverie for some time; at last he spoke abruptly:

"Sydenham, do you believe in a hell and in eternal punishment?"

"I do believe in the Bible, and in a state of future rewards and punishments," replied the other.

"So do I," said the Doctor. "This idea of some, that fear is not compatible with love, is not the true one. I think it not only is compatible, but necessary, even in the ordinary affairs of society, with a great majority of men. Strange that men will insist that fear of the divine punishment would utterly exclude love to God, when we know that the child loves its parent, but also feels some measure of fear in all cases, except where parents have entirely surrendered the reins of government."

"Yes," said Sydenham; "and take one step lower, to the brute creation. Take, for instance, the horse and dog, man's every-day companions; and any and every man accustomed to them well knows that the good horseman or hunter inspires both sentiments in his four-footed companion, and that the two are in no way incompatible."

"Still," said the Doctor, "the subject, doubtless, is not yet fully understood,"

"No," said the other, "and right there, in the unity of the two principles of love and fear, is locked up one of the greatest of human mysteries, or, rather, it is the key to unlock the wonders of God's government, and the great divine plan of love, justice and salvation."

The raft was just rounding a point where the river made a bend to the right, bearing to the west. The bluffs on each side were quite lofty, but while those on the right bank (or rather right-hand side of the river and back from the bank) were bathed in sunlight from base to summit, those on the left, cast their shadows two-thirds the way across the river, and touched the larboard side of the raft. Just opposite the raft, on the left bank, or Wisconsin side two Indian families had erected their lodges. The squaws were busied about the wigwams, while several Indian children were playing near, and a canoe with two Indians in it was approaching from down the river. As it drew near the sandy shore, the children started on a run to meet them, while the squaws followed more gravely to learn their success in fishing.

The perfectly tranquil river, the quiet and lofty hills, the shadow and sunlight, all formed a picture of beauty and peace ravishing to the senses, and long to be remembered. The raftsmen in following the channel happened for some time to be just on the line between the sunlight and shadow, and the effect was so beautiful and peculiar that all noticed it. Our friends watched the lengthening shadows gradually changing the beautiful scene in silence for some time. At length the Doctor remarked:

"What a pity that the Indians cannot be dealt with on the plain principles of common sense, justice and christianity! what is the matter? Those principles should guide the action of a great, free, liberal republic like ours."

"They are supposed to do so, "said Sydenham, "but they are obscured by demagoguism in politics, hypocrisy in religion, and sectionalism in both."

"Yes," said the Doctor, "that is too true. I remember in 1854 when the Kansas and Nebraska bill was under discussion in Congress, Senator Houston stated, substantially, that while it violated compromises that should be sacred, between the northern and southern people, it also VIOLATED A NUMBER OF SOLEMN TREATIES MADE BY THE WHOLE NATION WITH THE INDIANS INHABITING THOSE TERRITORIES."

"Very true," said Sydenham, "and yet that announcement made not the slightest impression either in Congress, or out of it[*].

"The political leaders," said the Doctor, "may not have been entirely destitute of respect for the treaties, and for the principles of justice; but they were determined (each party) upon maintaining positions that were most conspicuous and interesting to the people, to whom they looked for political preferment; and the people of both parties and sections were far more interested in the slavery question than they were in the fulfilment of compacts with each other, or treaties with the Indians."

"And yet," said Sydenham, "the great majority of the people of this nation wished the compromise measures and the Indian treaties, too, to stand,—to maintain and respect them, although their destroyers have gained promotion by their overthrow."

"Houston's words," said the Doctor, "will live in history, as the utterances of a true statesman and patriot; indeed, I believe the organization of those territories at

---

[*] "Washington's policy in regard to the Indians was always pacific and humane. He considered them as children, who should be treated with tenderness and forbearance. He aimed to conciliate them by good usage, to obtain their lands by fair purchase and punctual payments, to make treaties with them on terms of equity and reciprocal advantage, and strictly to redeem every pledge. In these respects he looked upon the Indian tribes as holding the same rank and the same rights as civilized nations. But their faithlessness, ravages and murders, were not to be tolerated, from whatever causes they arose."—*Spark's Life of Washington*, p 431,

all, at that time, to have been premature; we expend too fast in everything; far better is it to grow more slowly and more solidly."

"In 1854," said the other, "the political heat engendered by the Mexican war, the acquisition of territory, and the compromise of 1850, had not yet subsided. The great Clay was dead, and could not defend his noble work. His voice was heard no more in the Senate, but instead, were heard the voices of men of *almost* as great abilities, greater ambition and less principle. The heat and excitement, too, was not confined to the political world. The gold of California, followed swiftly by the great expansion of the railroad system, the building of cities, towns, &c., made that an exciting period in the social and business circles of the country; and the press and the pulpit were fired with ambition to lead, to govern, to be a part of the great and growing mass."

"In chemistry," said Sydenham, "certain tests may be applied to determine certain results; so in the moral and political world: the mass seems made up of so many different elements that it is hard to tell which predominates. Doubtless there was, and is, with many, a sincere belief that negro servitude is wicked and wrong, and some of this class may have a strong sense of justice toward particular classes, and some, or, possibly, a majority of all the people, may appreciate and wish to apply the principles of justice to *all;* yet, that these principles did not animate Congress, at that time, is clearly proved by the fact that no attention was paid to the Indian treaties; or, rather, that *after their attention was particularly called to them, they proceeded to deliberately trample them under foot.* One party professed great devotion to a principle—the principle of popular sovereignty; a principle sound in the main, but by no means infallible. And yet its supporters claimed nothing less than absolute infallibility for their pet, dogma—and that, with the example of Utah before their eyes."

"Were the perpetrators of the 'Mountain Meadows' massacre ever brought to justice?" enquired the other.

"No, not one of that infamous band were ever brought to justice. The government officials and the people could not see farther west than Kansas. As to the political parties, neither seemed to be alive to that fearful deed of blood, (in cruelty equaling and in treachery surpassing far the wild warfare of the savages) although most keenly alive to whatever might advance their chances of success in the elections. In the great crucible of American politics, the Kansas and Nebraska bill, therefore, furnishes for future historians a test. It proves that in neither political party was there a majority in Congress whose course was influenced solely by a desire to do right for its own sake, and that other motives and aims warped them from the straight and narrow path of truth."

The shades of night were now falling over the great river, and a call to supper ended the conversation between the two friends. After supper, however, it was resumed by Sydenham:

"Do you think, Doctor, that the compromise of 1850 was right and sufficient."

"'The scriptural axiom,'" said the Doctor, "'Sufficient for the day is the evil thereof,' is a good one in private affairs, and eminently wise in many great questions that arise in the affairs of governments.

"Time will always furnish a solution to many questions otherwise insoluble; men must labor, but they must also wait. The compromises of 1820 and of 1850 satisfied the people; but when they were overturned, the people were like an angry swarm of bees, and the Northern people were made to believe that slavery would spread, or might spread, throughout the territories; and the Southern people were led also to believe that the '*aggressive North*' would never let them take their negroes into any territory, and that the States where it existed would be so outnumbered and outvoted that they would never have any peace. Hence the desperate, disgraceful, foolish and wicked struggle in Kansas. Here was sown the fearful seed of dragon's teeth, which, as in the fable of old, I fear, will bring forth a crop of armed men. Had the compromise been allowed to stand, even until this time, it would have been very different. The lapse of time would at once have cooled the passions of the people, and afforded opportunity for arriving at more facts. The reaction of 1857 would have cooled the rage for speculation and emigration. The Indian question, and the Pacific railroad; the Pacific coast, and the trade of Asia, (each and all questions of vast practical moment) would have been brought forward, and would have furnished an ample field for the exercise of statesmanship, philanthropy and enterprise, in *fields most inviting and safe;* indeed, entirely free from the fearful dangers that must, inevitably, attend upon any rash measures or experiments with the slavery question. Ignoring history, revelation and present facts, there is a determination to make this a moral question; and, setting aside the practical issues involved, the theorists (both of abolition and propagandism), hesitate not to attack everything that lies in their path. Sectionalism never was so fierce, or party passion so strong, as now, while consideration for political opponents, and regard for the rights, feelings, and interests of each section by the other, is proportionately weak; indeed, the extremists of each section (the radicals), seem animated by intense malice and hatred against the other. Should these extremists get the lead, then God help the country; for fanaticism, violence and corruption will rule; and a fearful rule it is. The great majority of the people of the United States are conservative; yet they are liable to be misled—indeed they have already been misled by their trusted leaders, and if still farther misled, untoward circumstances may arise that will give the lead to these same extremists, and to ambitious demagogues; and then look out for a collision."

"And what after that?" said Sydenham.

"That is beyond mortal ken," said the Doctor; "but I should look for many evils, vast in magnitude, infinite in degree; even leaving out, altogether, the many valuable lives lost in battle, and by the fearful vicissitudes of war, for doubtless a terrible civil war, which would be one of the first and most appalling evils, would certainly follow the first collision."

"You mean the first collision of arms," said Sydenham.

"Yes," said the Doctor, "although a collision of the powers of the Federal and State Governments *might* occur and not be followed by a collision of arms. Such was the case in Jackson's time, in 1832, when, through the wisdom and patriotism of a few men, aided by some fortunate circumstances, a great calamity was averted. But now, unfortunately, there is a disposition to pervert the truth of history, and to make it appear that the array of force, and the influence of fear, were the sole agencies that were used to avert that great danger. This is an ungenerous and a dangerous error—an error in point of facts in the present state of the public mind, excited by sectional and party hate, (the political demagogues, hungry for the spoils of office) wise and patriotic councils would be at a discount; would not be acted upon, either in the North or South; and when once a collision of authority occurred, a collision of arms would follow; and this by a mighty war—a war, the heat and fury of which would (without the exercise of magnanimnity) be liable to *consume* the very qualities in the hearts of the people of regard for each other, and for public welfare, upon which the government rests. If this was all, it would be terrible for the *present* generation, but the *next* might revive the principles of christianity, and constitutional government, and rid itself of the corruption that would enter upon their overthrow. But the peculiar misfortune of civil wars is, that the succeeding generation reap the bitter fruit, and gather the fearful crop of hatred sown by their fathers."

"You take a gloomy view of the future," said Sydenham, "and I almost fear it may prove well founded; yet it would seem that such stupendous folly and crime belonged to the dark ages, and not to the middle of the nineteenth century."

"You are right," said the Doctor, "it would so seem, indeed; and," he added gravely, "I hope I will live to see that I have been only a visionary alarmist."

With this, the conversation ceased, and the friends sat in silent meditation. Near the stern or rear end of the raft, one of the men was playing on a violin. The night was calm and clear, but the moon had not yet risen; there was, however, a bright starlight. The forests upon the shores cast their dark shadows upon the river on each side, but in the middle was a lighter streak, which reflected upon its surface the stars overhead. Nature is often best enjoyed in silence; and the men sat looking upon the quiet river and its sombre shores for some time without a word.

"Do you remember, Doctor," said Sydenham, at length, "the words of Washington regarding magnanimity in affairs of state?"

"I do not know that I do," said the other: "what are they?"

"*There is an indissoluble union between a magnanimous policy and the solid rewards of public prosperity and felicity.*"

"There," said Sydenham, "is a christian mirror for the statesmen of the world: hold it up before nations, and what errors does it reveal? Hold it up before our own people, and our Congress, and see how given over to partisanship, personal ambition and sectionalism we have been."

Sydenham rose and led the way to their berths, and soon both were soundly sleeping. The group at the stern had already broken up and gone to bed; and, save an occasional word from the pilot and his watch, no sound of life came from the huge floating mass, as it drifted onward upon the swift current of the Mississippi.

CHAPTER XIV.

WHILE our raftsmen are drifting on past the beautiful towns and cities of the great States of Minnesota, Wisconsin, Iowa, Illinois and Missouri, which line the banks of the beautiful Upper Mississippi, and before they enter the turbid waters of the Lower Mississippi, we must leave them and change the scene of our story to a plantation on the banks of the lower river, in the State of Louisiana. It was in that fertile and beautiful delta known as "the Coast," a few miles below Baton Rouge, the capital of Louisiana, and only about fifty miles above New Orleans, the metropolis of the southwest. The river here is very different from where we left the raft, and so is the scenery. That was beautiful and grand, but a beauty and grandeur of a very different style. There were clear waters, rocks and towering bluffs. Here are dark and turbid waters, but a wide, deep and most noble river, very deep and free from rocks, snags and shoals. The shores are low, and the highest part is but a few rods back from the river. Here the famed "levees" are constructed; an embankment of earth reared upon the top of the little natural ridge near the river. From this the surface gradually descends, as you go back from the river, until, at the distance of from one to three miles, you reach the swamp. These lands are in the highest state of cultivation; or, rather, were at the time of which we write; and, as they had been so divided as to give every planter a front upon the river, while bounded in the rear by the swamp, the effect was to form almost a continuous village on each bank of the river, all the way up from New Orleans to Baton Rouge. Just inside the levee is the public road, and upon the road and river front the residences of the planters, with the groups of negro quarters, sugar mills, &c., near each. Beautiful groves and avenues of orange trees abound. The whole country is cultivated in sugar-cane, the delicate light green of which, forms a striking contrast with the sombre, and very dark-green foliage of the live-oak trees, which here and there dot the beautiful delta, or fringe its background.

We have said that the dwellings and business of the population and the public road was along the river bank. Nevertheless, the scene, while enlivened by the life of a quiet, yet strong and advancing civilization, population and power, was in no way robbed of the simplicity, beauty and grandeur which nature alone can give: for the great and majestic river, was the leading feature in the picture; and upon it man had wrought no change whatever. In times of great floods, indeed, its superabundant waters would be kept from extending far beyond their natural banks by the artificial levees; but at all other seasons (save that it bore upon its bosom the proud messengers of a mighty commerce) its deep and silent waters flowed onward to the sea in all the quiet majesty of nature.

At the time of which we write, it was a rich feast for the traveler, bound up from New Orleans, to take passage on one of the large and elegant Mississippi steamers that would leave that port in the morning. This would give an opportunity to see the beautiful panorama of "the coast" by daylight. From the upper deck you look down upon the shores; the land though highest near the river being lower than the upper deck. But back from the river the tops of the cane seem lower than the surface of the water. The effect of this is most pleasing and singular: you appear to be floating *above* the enchanting scenes of fairy land. The river is dark, wide and sombre. The country is below you, radiant in its mantle of pea-green, (the color of the sugar-cane) dotted and edged with the very dark foliage of the live-oak and cypress. The river, a full mile or more in width, bears upon its broad bosom many large steamers, and other water craft, and upon its shores a teeming population.

But enough of description: our business is with one family in this southern land—this hive of sweets, and, we may add, of industry and thrift. The plantation is one of about the average size, and the buildings are not larger or more costly than the average planters' residences on the coast. Everything is in good order, as is usual here; and considerable taste has been shown in the grounds about the mansion, in the planting of shrubbery and trees, and in the general arrangement of the place. The negro quarters are neat and comfortable; and by day are enlivened by the voices and gambols of children, and at night by the songs, chatter and merry-making of the adult colored people of both sexes. The residence is surrounded by wide and airy verandas, and has a most comfortable and homelike appearance, but by no means pretentious or ostentatious. Its "expression," as Downing would say, is of quiet, of comfort and of open hospitality. Nor does this outside appearance at all mislead; for tranquil, peaceful, innocent enjoyment of life, adorned by the genuine virtues of kindness, integrity, hospitality and faith are the characteristics of its inmates.

Henry Barrona, the owner of this place, was born of French and English parents, in this country, and had been living in this very house about twenty-five years. His father, Pierre Barrona, had left France during the horrors of the "reign of terror," after the beginning of the revolution, and, after many wanderings, had finally come to New Orleans, about the year 1800. Here, not long after, he had married an English lady, the widow of an enterprising young English merchant, who had recently come out from England, and had fallen a victim to the yellow fever. Barrona belonged to an old and wealthy family of France, but, as his parents died about the beginning of the revolution, and as he had no brothers or sisters, he formed the determination never to return; and after his marriage in New Orleans, (then an insignificant town) devoted himself to mercantile pursuits. A fine specimen of the French gentleman of the old school, chivalrous and generous, with all the vivacity of his race, and its high sense of honor. He was most ardently attached to his wife, whose tranquil virtues and patient thoughtfulness of every duty in life were in strong contrast with her impulsive husband.

Here Henry was born, and afterward two daughters, one of whom died young, while the other (Margaret) married a planter on the coast, and lived only about three miles from her brother.

Henry Barrona quite early showed a distaste for the life of a merchant, and, on the death of his father, came up on the coast and settled on land his father had purchased. Educated in the most careful manner, by the most careful parents, and especially by the most devoted mother, young Barrona did not altogether relish the society of the fashionable circles in New Orleans, nor of the coast, at that time; and soon after his plantation was improved, leaving it in the hands of an overseer, he spent several years traveling in Europe, in the north of Africa, in Egypt and in Palestine. On his return from the East he spent some months in Spain, and there married, under singular and romantic circumstances, (of which we must give a sketch) a daughter of that sunny land.

Juan Pinzon, of Seville, a man who, had circumstances favored, might have become famous, was one of that numerous class, all the world over, who have to struggle through life for a subsistence.

Every one knows that bull-fighting is a national amusement in Spain; that thousands gather to witness these gladiatorial contests of man against brute.

Pinzon was a bull-fighter from necessity, and fought the bulls for the people's amusement, because by it he could gain his bread, Nevertheless, though a poor matadore, he won the love of a high-born Castilian beauty, the daughter of a house possessing a stock of pride sufficient for a nation, if distributed out in small parcels. Fearful was the rage and fury when she eloped with the matadore. But in another city they dwelt in safety, and Juan pursued his trade, hazarding his life for a support for his fondly loved wife. His devoted wife loved him as only a Spanish woman can love; but the burthen of disgrace and disinheritance heaped upon her by her family were too much, and she died when her first-born and only child was but ten years old. The poor matadore, whose life had been gloriously brightened by the love of this self-sacrificing, beautiful and affectionate woman, (who was of that kind of whom Irving says: "one of the most gifted and fascinating beings I ever met with, even among the fascinating daughters of Spain,") was almost heartbroken at his loss, but soon transferred all his earthly affections to his beautiful child; and, as she grew in years, the more, to her father's eye, she resembled her mother, and the more she absorbed the gushing affection of his soul. Rejecting, with a scorn embittered by the thought of his wife's long grief, all offers from her family to adopt his daughter as their own, he managed out of his scanty earnings to provide for and educate her in a manner befitting her talents and beauty. And Isabella Pinzon was beautiful, even in Spain—that land of female loveliness. Her father had watched her with most jealous care; and her filial affection, heightened by companionship, and a knowledge of the fearful danger of his life, caused her to love her father as few fathers are loved, and to reject the advances of suitors whom he disapproved.

It was at Cadiz that young Barrona first saw and loved this beautiful girl. It was not long after seeing her at the cathedral that he sought out her father at his humble lodgings, and asked permission to wait upon his daughter. Pinzon was pleased with the manly foreigner, and well knew the difference between this man of honor and the butterflies of fashion against whom he had kept strict watch over his pearl; and after he had become satisfied through a commercial house of the standing of Barrona, he had introduced him to his daughter, to whom he paid his addresses. But Isabella Pinzon rejected his offer. She knew little of the world; and the American did not win her love. Yet she treated him kindly, though her eyes rested longer on the gay and dashing cavaliers of Cadiz. They were gallant in appearance, and looked brave, if not heroic; and she could discover nothing heroic in the rather modest Barrona, who possessed much of his mother's gentleness. Naturally enough, she did not appreciate him, nor did he know the mysterious secrets of a woman's heart. As she treated him with gentle kindness, her father hoped she would yet learn to love him. It was on the occasion of a great tournament that all this was changed, and a great grief came upon her.

Her father was considered one of the best bull-fighters in Spain; yet he preferred fighting the bulls on foot, and always dreaded the dangers of the arena on horseback. On this occasion the fete was to be one of extraordinary magnificence. A wild bull of remarkable size and ferocity had been procured, and Pinzon, assisted by two others, was to fight him on horseback.

Isabella knew the danger of her father in these encounters; but from her childhood he had rarely been hurt, and she had no fears. A gay young gallant had invited her to accompany him to the amphitheatre, and, against her father's wishes, though not against his commands, she had accepted his invitation.

The amphitheatre was one of the finest in Spain; the audience was brilliant; on all sides of the arena was a blaze of beauty and fashion.

The signal was given, and in galloped the matadores. Her father at the head elicited the praise of all. Another signal, and the bull is released, and with a furious bellow rushed into the ring. The other matadores pierced him with their lances to increase his fury, and then, when his rage was greatest, the signal was given to evade him no longer, but begin the attack. Pinzon urged his horse forward, but frightened at the size and fury of the bull, the steed shied and reared upon his hind legs. In an instant the bull was upon him, and horse and rider were rolled in the dirt. Pinzon's form was hidden for a moment, but the next revealed to the spectators that the horse, impaled upon the horns of the bull, had fallen upon him, and the bull was fiercely goring both. The other matadores could not bring their horses to the attack, and a moment more would decide the fate of the man. Piercing screams from the ladies were heard on all sides. Young Barrona, snatching a sword and cloak from a Spanish gallant near him, who had leveled his opera glass critically upon the brutal scene, sprang into the arena. Instantly every sound was hushed. Barrona paused not for an instant, but bounded quickly to the side of the bull, and plunged the blade into him. The monster turned with a roar of pain, and Barrona struggled in vain to recover his blade. It broke in the middle. The hot breath of the enraged brute was upon him. Hurling the cloak, it caught by a lucky chance over his horns, and for a moment blinded him. That moment was enough: the stroke he had received was mortal, and he soon reeled and then fell. The amphitheatre resounded with applause. Barrona gave no further thought to the bull, but rushed to rescue the unfortunate Pinzon. Isabella was already there. The matadores and assistants removed the dying horse, and Isabella and Barrona kneeled beside the dying man. Skillful surgeons were soon in attendance, and, to the anxious question of Barrona, answered that he had not long to live, certainly not but a few hours. Yet, in spite of his fearful injuries, and the sudden and terrible shock, the unfortunate man was perfectly conscious. His upturned eyes had rested on Barrona when he dealt the deadly thrust to the bull; he had seen his peril and his deliverance, and he had marked the burning glance of gratitude and admiration the weeping daughter of his heart had cast upon her rejected suitor, as they knelt beside him. Pinzon, although a bull-fighter from necessity, was a most gallant, devoted, brave and sagacious man. He knew that his daughter was possessed of a noble soul, and that Barrona was every way worthy of her; and it had grieved him very greatly that the American's quiet and gentle ways had caused him to be outshone by the dashing but really worthless cavaliers of Cadiz. Besides, he knew that Barrona was wealthy, or at least possessed of a competency, and that he could place his darling beyond the reach of that blighting poverty that her devoted mother had borne for him, and with which he had all his life struggled: for Pinzon would always tell his family and friends, when allusion was made to his profession, that it was poverty and not the bulls that he was fighting. So now the poor matadore, after periling his life for many years to support his loved ones, and having passed through dangers innumerable almost unscathed, meeting at length his terrible fate, sees the hope revealed through that same stroke of the fulfilment of his dearest earthly wishes. He was borne away kindly and tenderly to his little home; and Isabella, with her beauteous face bathed in tears, ministered to him with all the wild devotion of despair. Pinzon suffered fearful agony, but his soul was roused to its highest and noblest powers, and, despite his agony, he longed to know that his wishes would be realized, and his child given in marriage to so true and brave a man. When all had gone save the physician, the priest and Barrona, the dying man signified his wish to be alone with his daughter. Silently they withdrew, and Pinzon took the hand of his weeping girl in his own.

"My daughter," said he, "child of your sainted mother, I will soon die, and you will be left alone in a selfish and wicked world. Tell me, child, which one of these Cadiz gallants do you love, and who will offer you his hand when you are alone and friendless in the world?"

"I love none of them, my father; they are all selfish and base cowards, who would have let the bull gore you to death. I despise them all," sobbed the poor girl.

A smile of gladness lighted the matadore's bronzed face. "And what of the American," he asked, "do you still despise him? He will soon sail for the New World."

"Despise him!" said Isabella, "Oh, no, dear father; I could not despise the noblest and bravest man in Cadiz."

"My child, could I give you to him before I die, I should be happy. Tell me, will you not love him?"

"I do now love him, my father," said Isabella, "but he will leave me after what has passed."

Pinzon motioned for the door to be opened, and for the others to approach, and there, in the presence of the dying man, the weeping girl was betrothed. There were no dry eyes there; even the old Spanish surgeon, who had witnessed human agony on the battlefield, and in every form, wept tears of sorrow and of joy, while the venerable priest fervently blessed the weeping pair.

A moment more, and Pinzon, embracing fervently his beloved daughter, and grasping the hand of Barrona, motioned them back, and then the last rites of the church were administered. This done, Pinzon motioned Isabella and Barrona to join hands, and taking their clasped hands in both of his, they kneeling by his bedside, he with his last words invoked the blessing of God upon this union and upon their posterity. His voice then sunk to a whisper, and Isabella could only distinguish the name of her dead mother. A few moments more, and the soul of the matadore had winged its flight.

The Cadiz journals were filled with accounts of the

death of the most celebrated bull-fighter in Spain, and the family of Isabella Pinzon's mother soon heard of her father's death, and sent to ask her to come and live with them; and this, by the advice of Barrona and the good priest, she finally did; and there, some months later, the marriage was solemnized; and Barrona soon after sailed for America with his bride. Soon after reaching New Orleans his father died, and he then removed with his wife and mother to the plantation; and here Isabella Pinzon Barrona, the character we will now introduce to the reader, was born. She was now almost twenty years of age, a fully matured woman, rather tall, of a graceful form of almost faultless proportions. She was indeed most beautiful, but her beauty was rather of the Spanish type, more than French, English or American, though all were somewhat blended. It was in her character and manners that Isabella happily illustrated the blending of these nationalities; in the vivacity of the French, the stability and dignity of the English, the practical originality and adaptation to circumstances of the American, and the warm affection and devotion of the Spanish woman. Inheriting piety and religious faith, it was with her a fixed principle, and a part of her nature, not yet, however, sublimated and refined by suffering and trial to that high degree that maturer years would bring; yet love to God, and love and charity for all mankind, had been instilled into her mind from infancy; and her generous nature developed the seeds of pure instruction, so that now her full and generous soul beamed from her eyes, and spoke in every word and act and look. To minister to the sick, the suffering and the poor, was with her no hard task, performed only from a sense of duty, and leaving behind a painful sense of meritorious conduct and great righteousness on her part. Noble and generous impulses were with her like a perennial spring, bursting from the rock of a lofty faith and pure character, refreshing everything it touched, happy in the good deeds that made others happy. The negroes on the plantation looked upon her as a kind of ministering angel, and their love was tempered by reverence and resepct. Happy and contented with their lot, (for they had a kind master) there was rarely much suffrying to alleviate; yet the sick always expected and received a visit from the "young missus," the prelude always of delicacies and supplies sent for their use. Her life had been beset by few crosses and trials, and her spirit was joyous and free, and yet thoughtful and contemplative. Compared with the gay butterflies of fashion, she would have seemed a sage. Well acquainted with the languages of her parents and grandparents, she had read under the tutelage of her father many of the choicest works in the English, French and Spanish languages, and was well grounded in history and science. Graceful in her movements and bearing, with eyes dark, lustrous and expressive, the great poet's words might fitly be applied:

"Grace in her form, Heaven in her eye,
In every movement dignity and love."

Such was our heroine. Nature had done much for her, and the fortunate circumstances of her life, and education under the eyes of a careful mother, and a father who knew the world, had done more. The cold, chilling breath of poverty had never blown upon her ardent and impulsive nature, nor had the opposite influences of wealth and fashion ever corroded her soul. She had been taught respect for her parents in all things; and this had done much to prevent her affections being fixed, ere the time of which we write, upon some unworthy object. Her mother had told her, over and over again, the story of her girlhood, and of her own narrow escape from all the ills of misplaced love; of the terrible death of her father, her discovery of the baseness of her lover, and the worth of Barrona; of her instant and full-grown love, even in that fearful moment; of her dying father's devotion and heroism, in securing and confirming their betrothal when in the very throes of death; of her sorrow, and all the strange, sad, unwonted incidents of that most singular and hallowed period of her life, in which grief and love so strongly and so sacredly joined.

CHAPTER XV.

THE other characters in this southwestern home are quickly sketched. They are the younger children.

Pierre, named after his grandfather, a fine and manly youth of seventeen; and Mary, a daughter of fourteen, in whom appeared more of the English cast of features of her grandmother than was shown by her elder sister.

Pierre was now at home from his first college vacation, and the younger daughter was to be sent to an institution in St. Louis, the following autumn.

Both parents were fond of reading and study; and the Spanish woman, under the tuition of her husband, had amply made amends for the deficiency of her younger days. Barrona attended carefully and diligently to business, in all its plans, arrangments and details, but as this was done *every day*, so every day gave him also sufficient time for study, social intercourse, open air exercise and the family circle. With the lady of the house the same excellent order and division of time prevailed, and a home that was indeed "*sweet*" was the result. Here flourished the genuine virtues and pleasures of life, and religion was their handmaid. Very little attention was paid to fashion. They rarely visited the city, but the climate obliged them to go almost every season, for a period, away from the malaria of the swamps. And this season they had proposed an extended tour, and for the first time to visit St.

Paul, which they could do by embarking for that purpose on a steamer at the landing near their sugar-mill, and with a single change at St. Louis, disembarking at St. Paul. On this trip they were soon to embark; and the daughters and son, who had long been promised this, to them, extraordinary recreation and grand summer tour, were in a fever of anticipation and excitement. Barrona, who was a "traveled man," looked with pleasure upon this delightful expectation on the part of the younger members of his family, and that of his sister who were to accompany him. Of this sister and her family we must now say a few words.

Julia Barrona was the only sister of Henry, and married, during her father's lifetime, a northern merchant named Johnson, who had suffered a commercial shipwreck of his fortune and business in one of the numerous financial revulsions to which our country seems almost as much subject as South America is to earthquakes. Sick and disgusted with the world, he went to New Orleans, where his capacity and integrity and steadfast sterling character soon won him many friends, and where he in a few years retrieved his affairs. A warm friendship existed between him and the elder Barrona, which seemed also to descend to the daughter, whom he wooed and won, and they were married, on her brother's return from the old world. Succeeding well in commercial pursuits, he yet was not content to pass his life in the turmoil and risk of commerce; and, some time after his brother-in-law had settled on "the coast," he too bought a plantation a few miles below, and, closing up all his business in the city, he began the quiet life of a planter. Here, after some years of happy domestic life, he died of yellow fever, about five years before the period of our story, leaving his wife, a daughter and son, possessed of a handsome fortune. Amelia Johnson was now in her eighteenth year, while her brother Thomas was in his sixteenth. Wealthy, and deprived of a father's guidance while so young, certainly, it was by no means strange if they were somewhat possessed of those objectionable characteristics of the children of so many wealthy parents, who are neglected or spoiled by over-indulgence: and yet the sterling qualities of father and mother asserted themselves, and they strictly obeyed their gentle mother, who in her widowhood governed her family, her home and plantation, with discretion, ability and dignity, assisted of course by the counsel and advice of her brother. Amelia was a beautiful girl, Anglo-American in appearance and character, with fair complexion, blue eyes and auburn hair, amiable and less impassioned and enthusiastic than her half-Spanish cousin, Isabella, yet withal more self-willed and wayward. Her brother was a promising boy, but rather slight and delicate in form—not robust, as if reared in a purer and more bracing atmosphere. The mother, Mrs. Johnson, was now thirty-eight years of age, and was a handsome and highly interesting lady, of excellent head and heart, and looked forward to the Minnesota tour with as much pleasurable anticipation as did her children, and even more; for it would be a relief from the constant care of the plantation, which, since her husband's death, devolved upon her, and which had been like the government of a little kingdom. Like Penelope, too, it furnished her the means of escape from importunate suitors, which, from the earliest ages, no wealthy, amiable and handsome widow has ever been without.

Of Barrona we must now say a few more words. He was now at that time of life when the reflective powers are strongest, and judgment best. Singularly generous and magnanimous in disposition, he yet knew enough of the world to be wary and cautious in great and important affairs; yet he was always open, frank and genial. A Catholic by education, he was by no means a bigot, or a blind follower of priestly guidance; but, taught by his gentle English mother, he drew his faith from the pure fountain of the gospel, and knew that in love to God, and love to man, was found the only religious character truly worthy. So in politics he drew his opinions from the teachings of history, the study of the writings of the founders of our government, and the analysis of its structure and of present and settled facts. Such a man could not of course be a sectarian in religion, or a sectionalist in politics; and Barrona was neither. He was a christian, and loved his Maker and his Saviour, and revered his word. He was an American, and reverenced the constitution and laws of his country, and despised its demagogues. And so very naturally he found himself without a church, and without a party, and so, far less popular (though none the less respected) than he would otherwise have been. And maintaining thus his integrity, he had kept aloof from all political ambition, and enjoyed the quiet of his home; but the days were coming when he could no longer do this. Plain and unostentatious in his style of living and personal expenditures, his wealth was used with a free hand to promote the advancement of all worthy objects; and no worthy person in need ever went " empty away" from him. To the pride of wealth, of position, of family, or of section, he was a stranger. His greatest pride was pride of character—of a line of conduct governed by the rule of right, and the principles of conscientious, honorable behavior—and even this was always held in check by his religious feelings, christian humility, and charity for the errors of others. The character of his wife had in the lapse of time assimilated greatly with his own. The impassioned Spanish girl had now become the staid matron, presiding over her household with kindness, dignity and grace, and always the solace and companion of her husband, leaning on him, and yet strengthening his strength, and aiding to purify his character by her love.

Having now sketched these two families, and something of this most highly interesting part of what was once known as the southwest, we will return to our friends on the raft.

CHAPTER XVI.

WITH the advancing season, the voyage on the Upper Mississippi became more and more pleasant and interesting, and to the Doctor, (accustomed to a southern climate) the greater degree of warmth was more agreeable, and the trip more and more enjoyable And the Doctor did, indeed, find very great pleasure in these quiet days and nights, floating down the noble river. But it was not an idle, listless, sensual pleasure. His mind was occupied with profound reflections, (some of which he committed to writing) and from this continual pressure of thought, reading and conversation was a relief.

As for Sydenham, he had his constant round of duties in managing his raft, relieved greatly, however, by the enjoyment of the scenery, and by reading and conversation with his friend, (the Doctor) and the men on the raft.

But that was a period when thoughtful men feared national trouble, and a cloud of anxiety for the political future rested upon both the friends, which, although they continually reasoned away, would return whenever they obtained newspapers from the passing steamers, and saw reflected there indications of the sectional hatred and party passion that seemed to continually increase. They talked of these things often, in the quiet nights and long and calm afternoons, (never in anger) but the future they could not foresee and realize And happy is it for mortals that the future is unknown; that the coming days and months and years are curtained from our view. But while not one hour of the future can we claim, the past is all our own—that is, its teachings are at our command; its wisdom and experience are the store-houses to which we may always resort. Thus, history calls us back from theories that we fancy new, and shows us their counterpart in the dim and misty past. Science does, indeed, seem to progress forward in many things, while in others it moves, as it were, in a circle: yet who shall say what arts of the past have been lost, or what of the present may not be? But, however this may be, certain it is that the *nature of man* does not change, and that the human heart is, to-day, as with the first man and woman created upon the planet. The vicissitudes of all recorded human history show the perfect correctness through thousands of years, and up to the present hour, of the delineation of man in the Revealed Word. And there is not, on all the crags and battlements and ruins that line the highway of the past, in all the world's literature, from Homer down, a hope hung out, save only in that Word and in the Gospel of Christ, that shines in its pure effulgence like a mountain of diamonds in the weary waste. And yet, how frightfully perverted; what crimes have been committed; what woes heaped upon mankind in its name. Well might Voltaire scoff, and point the finger of scorn at deeds done in the name of Christianity that would make a Pagan blush. What candid student of the past will deny this? What candid and unbiassed student of the present (if any such there be), will deny its follies, sins, hypocrisies and dangers? And, greatest of all its dangers, is HYPOCRISY! And where must we seek the path of truth and safety? This world, hung in the mighty vault of space, was not left without laws to guide its flying course, and direct its diurnal motion. So in the moral world. Man, created the highest inhabitant of the planet, and but a little lower than the angels, was not left a prey to his own natural passions and impulses; left a free agent, his Creator guided him, or pointed the way. The awful sublimity of the book of Genesis can only be rightly appreciated by rising upon the wings of the mind, (the imagination) placing ourselves in the vast realms of space, and turning our eyes upon the earth, unfinished and crude; passing through those wonderful stages until creation was finished and time began, and the first pair, in their glorious beauty, stood before their Creator and Lord. Then began the contest between right and wrong; between evil and good; between a little knowledge and supreme wisdom; between unrestrained liberty and necessary subjection.

The period of man's direct intercourse with God has indeed passed, but his word remains; the record and the law have been wonderfully and mysteriously preserved. Left through God's providence in the hands of the highest races of men; and now, through the art of printing, steam and electricity, with all the aids of civilization, art, and human power, why may not the divine guide be distributed through and adopted, at least by the civilized christian world, and the Gospel be received by the nations in sincerity? Simply because man's nature is prone to err; and the human heart is, to-day, as in that of the first man, and worse; for his little stock of knowledge has filled his heart; has made him now wear God's word as a cloak, under which he sows the Devil's seed, and calls it "law," or "liberty," as will best suit his purpose. This age does not revere God's word, nor does it respect the historic annals of the human race. Neither the teachings of revelation or of history are studied or respected now by the masses, or by a majority of the educated. This is the age of the *theorist*, in morals, in government, in religion.

The modern preacher seems to have little or no humility. Unlike St. Paul, who feared that he might, at last be a castaway, the modern preacher seems to have no doubts, no humility; on the contrary, he seems to almost feel that he may, himself, prescribe the terms of salvation. He does not so much insist on the merit, truth and excellence of the Gospel itself, as the truth and power of his own deduction therefrom. Indeed, though he generally patronizes the Bible, he feels obliged, sometimes, to apologize for it, especially where it seems to conflict with cherished theories of his own. In such cases, he generally seeks out carefully, and presents those particular passages that seem to sustain his point; carefully omitting, like a skillful lawyer, everything that makes against it. In this way he gains credit for great ability.

CHAPTER XVII.

THEY had now left Minnesota behind, and were approaching the southern confines of Wisconsin, having the State of Iowa on the right, or west bank of the river. The character of the scenery had changed, the hills being less lofty. At Dunleith, the north-west corner of Illinois, they landed for the first time in some hundreds of miles. From this point a great line of railway, the "Illinois Central," leads south-east and then south, through the centre of the State to Cairo, at the confluence of the Ohio and Mississippi rivers. At the north-western terminus three great States unite—Iowa, Wisconsin and Illinois, so, at the southern—Illinois, Missouri and Kentucky, separated only by the width of the river. This great work, with its "Chicago Branch," leading from Centralia to Chicago, in all, seven hundred miles in length, has performed, and is destined to perform a most important part in the development of all the vast country, whose wants it accommodates—a splendid triumph of healthy advancement creditable to the genius of Rantoul, the statesmanship of Douglas, to the State, and the west, and to numerous eminent men connected with it. The first great and complete success of the kind, it has been most fruitful in promoting others, and, by its successful precedent, and the connections offered by its completed trunks, aiding greatly in the establishment of that great and extended system of railways which now penetrates and interlocks these vast areas of the west—the heart of the continent.

After a few hours in Dunleith, and Dubuque, which lies just opposite, on the Iowa side of the river, they shoved off and proceeded on their voyage. Just before they started, a passenger came on board who wished to go down the river a few miles to a point near Galena, Ill., where he resided. The Doctor and he were soon enjoying a smoke together, and a pleasant acquaintance, western fashion, was soon established between the stranger, Doctor Ross and Sydenham. He had been an officer in the U. S. Army, was educated at West Point, and had served in the Mexican war. The conversation turned upon politics, and he expressed his preference for Douglas for the Presidency in the ensuing fall election, and his fears of the future if he should be defeated. He also expressed, in strong terms, condemnation of the radicals of both sections. To while away the time, the Doctor produced a pack of cards, and a few social games of euchre were played; but there was no betting. Soon they arrived at the landing for Galena, and Sydenham sent his skiff out to land his passenger, with whom they parted with mutual expressions of friendly regard. How wild a dream would then have seemed the events in which this man was to play so important a part in the near future.

For nearly six hundred miles now (as the river flows,) it bounds the State of Illinois upon the west, while Iowa and Missouri are upon the opposite side. At this time there were not so many railroad bridges crossing the river to accommodate the great lines stretching westward, as at present; but at Rock Island there was one that was an object of some dread to steamboatmen, and of great dread to raftsmen, many serious accidents having happened there. Sydenham had never passed through this bridge, and naturally felt much anxiety about it. Seth Lane, his pilot, had passed it a few times, and had once struck the pier, damaging his raft. From Galena down, the bridge and its passage was uppermost in the thoughts and conversation of all on the raft. Arrived near the head of the rapids, the wind blowing rather hard, the raft was moored to the bank until it snould subside. The next morning at daybreak, the wind having gone down, the lines were cast off and preparations made for "running the rapids," and "shooting the bridge."

This bridge having been a subject of great controversy between the river men and railroad men of the west, and also between the cities of Chicago and St. Louis, (the one the river, and the other the railroad metropolis) a brief description of it may not be uninteresting; and it is interesting because it is the *first* bridge that ever spanned the "Father of Floods."

From the Illinois shore to the island there is a causeway. The bridge proper, then, is built across the main channel of the Mississippi, from Rock Island to the Iowa shore. There is, at this point, a rocky ledge or "chain," extending across the bed of the river, known to river men as the "foot" of the Upper Rapids of the Mississippi. On this the bridge is built. The rapids extend from about two miles below Port Byron, (some twenty miles above) to this point, and throughout this extent the current of the river is very swift; and when the water is at a low stage, there are some dangerous places. The bridge is built of wood on stone piers, with a draw resting on a round central pier on which it is made to turn. When turned, the open space for the passage of steamers, &c., is one hundred and twenty feet. There is, also, a frame work of timber extending up and down from the central and side piers of the draw for the protection both of the bridge and passing vessels; and, as piles could not be driven, this is fastened to the rocky bottom. In this, it is said, the engineer made a mistake, in not studying the current sufficiently, and getting these guards exactly parallel with the central line of current. Certain it is, many accidents occurred here, until this was remedied; and from these rose much litigation for damages, contention and bitterness. Perhaps neither side were sufficiently considerate of the rights of the other. The utility of railroads and the necessity of bridging navigable rivers is not to be questioned; but the RIVERS AND LAKES are the people's highways, and, in the language of the *truly great* statesman of 1789, should be " forever free."

The river men, then, very properly were jealous of any obstruction to the navigation of the river, and the railroad men, with equal propriety, insisted that railroad bridges must be built to accommodate the great lines to be extended west. These views on both sides were just and reasonable, and *perfectly capable of being harmonized and reconciled*, as are many other dogmas that *seem* to conflict; but of course there were in this, as in other great questions, many extremists, radicals and irreconcilables on both sides: hence the trouble,—expensive and hurtful to every interest save the lawyers engaged.

As we have said, our raftsmen cast off their line at the head of the rapids, some twenty miles above, at the first grey of morning, and soon found themselves in much swifter water than they had yet found. On right merrily they glided, rapidly passing trees, bluffs and other landmarks. The river was now up, the high water removing all apprehension of sunken rocks; the bridge was the only cause of solicitude.

"If we had such a stream as this," said the Doctor, "all the way, we would soon reach Louisiana."

"Yes," said Sydenham, laughing, "but it would take me a long time *to get back*, and steamboating would then be a slower business than rafting."

"I do n't think we could alter or change the works of nature so as to make an improvement," said the Doctor.

"No," said one of the men (Sandy) "but the Akansaw man, running for office, told his constituents that if they would only elect him to Congress he would *try;* that he would unscrew all creation, take it apart, clean it and put it together again."

"That," said the Doctor, "would seem to bear some resemblance to the ancient fable of the presumptuous youth who would drive the chariot of the sun, instead of Apollo."

"It will do for a kind of Americanization of the old fable," said Sydenham, "and should be set down in the Arkansas classics."

"Seriously,' said the Doctor, "some people will not grow wiser by experience, and have done with vagaries; for many popular fancies do not even come up to the dignity of theories. They are vagaries, and vagaries only, morbid, diseased and unhealthy."

"Were wagons a thing of which the people had only heard and read, and heard explained and discussed, I think it by no means certain that it would be generally agreed that four wheels was the proper number. I have no doubt that there would be found a large party advocating the advantages of six wheels, another in favor of five, and still another in favor of having only three wheels to a wagon."

After the laughter occasioned by this sally had subsided, the Doctor continued:

"Moreover, I have no doubt that as good arguments and as much eloquence would be displayed by either the six, five, or three-wheeled party as by that in favor of four wheels; and, though it should be shown by the four-wheeled party that the other vehicles had been tried in some remote part of the world, several thousand years ago, and had failed, yet nothing short of a full and thorough trial would satisfy them to the contrary of their opinions."

"The first trial, however, would end the matter," said one of the listeners.

"I think not," said the Doctor, with a smile. "We will suppose that before any were tried the whole subject had been agitated for a time. The speculator is only a step behind the theorist, and sometimes even gets ahead. Before any trial could be entirely conclusive and generally admitted to be so, there would be no village, town or city, where some one would not be interested in the pecuniary way in the success of the new vehicles, and, long after four wheels had won the day, in the larger towns, three and five-wheeled vehicles would be the style in the remote settlements of Iowa and Kansas, and even the pavements of Boston and other large cities would long resound with the odd numbers driven by some plucky speculators in those machines, who would not give it up."

"That would be called an extreme view," said Sydenham.

"I saw ship-loads of things sent to California," said one of the men, "that were of no more use than the fifth wheel to a wagon."

"Not so much," said another listener, "for the fifth wheel *might* be taken along as an *extra*, and used in case one of the others break down, whereas *no possible use* could be made of hundreds of contrivances we saw in California in '49 and '50, sent there from Boston."

The attention of all hands was now called to some work on the raft, and the conversation ceased. The raft dashed swiftly along, while Sydenham and the pilot talked of the passage of the bridge. Soon they came in sight of it; a long train from Chicago, bound westward, was just entering upon the causeway from the Illinois shore. It rolled onward, and soon more than thirty cars followed the iron horse out over the rapid river. It was a grand sight, and all looked upon it intently; the outlines of the train, locomotive and its cloud of smoke cut sharply against the sky beyond. Viewed from the raft, right upon the surface of the river above, the sight was more striking than from any other point. Soon it reached the Iowa shore; and now all were absorbed with another passage, and to them more important. Sydenham stood by the side of the pilot: not a word was spoken while the rushing flood hurried them on. Now they are close to the bridge—now under it—now clear—not yet; the stern is drawn by the mighty current toward the pier, and all the efforts of the men cannot prevent a collision. It strikes and grates sharply; boards are broken and some torn out, but now they are clear below the bridge and the rapid; the raft is not broken or much damaged. Now bend to the sweeps to clear her of the eddy on the Illinois side. Soon this is passed; then all breathe freely, and go to work to repair damages. Some lumber is gone and some displaced and broken, and Sydenham is advised to make his claim for damages against the railroad company, but well aware of the delay, difficulty, annoyance and expense of this resort, he prefers not to do so; thinks it cheaper to lose it.

Davenport, Iowa, and Rock Island, Illinois, both fine little cities, are soon passed, and by afternoon the raft has become quiet and monotonous as usual.

CHAPTER XVIII.

THE general course of the river which, from Lake Pepin, and, indeed, from a point far above the falls of St. Anthony, is south-easterly, changes near Savannah, Illinois, to a more southerly course, which it holds past the towns of Fulton, Lyons and Clinton, then south-westerly, then south to about the head of the rapids, from whence to Muscatine it runs almost west: then a sharp angle, and it runs almost south to Port Louisa; thence it bears east, then south to Oquowka, thence southwesterly, past Burlington, Fort Madison and other places to Nauvoo and Montrose, thence south to Keokuk, at the foot of what is known as the lower rapids. Here it receives a large tributary from Iowa, Des Moines river, and between here and Quincy reaches its most westerly point of the great bend to the west, giving the State of Illinois here its greatest breadth. From this point it flows south-easterly until a few miles from the mouth of the Illinois, when it turns and runs a *north-easterly* course to the point of junction, where it receives the quiet waters of that river, when it again pursues a south-easterly course to the mouth of the Missouri. The union of these great rivers entirely changes the character of the Mississippi. For some distance its waters do not mingle with the tide waters of the Missouri, but keep to the Illinois side, as though shunning the embrace. At last, however, the whole volume of waters becomes charged with the earthy water, never again to become clear until far out upon and mingled with the deep waters of the great sea.

The Upper Mississippi, although having these graceful curves and bends, which are its "lines of beauty," is by no means a crooked river, as compared with its course below the junction with the Missouri, from which point, though swiftly going southerly to the Gulf of Mexico, it seems to be continually turning around, as though the "Father of Waters" was engaged in a waltz. Searching its way through the deep, rich, alluvial bottoms, changing its channel, filling up in a single season on one side with vast sandy deposits, while removing solid acres (covered with great trees) upon the other side, thus continually changing its borders and channel, yet, after all, remaining unchanged in all its essential characteristics, typifying the changes of matter and of spirit, while struggling with the finite on its way toward the infinite, and at last to be poured into the great ocean of eternity; yet never to be lost. Thus the great river rolls its waters toward the sea.

But we are still between the upper and lower rapids, and must not get ahead of our time, on the great float which now bears us onward. Of the river-towns which we have passed and are now passing, many are very handsome and thriving, and much of the country is in some places well improved, and adorned with neat and handsome homes, but yet the country contiguous to the river is not esteemed so rich or favorable for agriculture as that further back. The bottom lands are, of course, rich, but of this a great part is in forest, and subject to overflow. The great agricultural wealth is in the prairies, back of the broken and comparatively poor lands of the river bluffs. These bluff lands, however, are in many places esteemed good; indeed, in some places very superior for the culture of fruit, grapes, &c. Coal is generally abundant and easily accessible. Stone is also generally convenient, and abundant for building purposes, and there are many quarries of very superior quality. At the rapids there is a large waterpower which at Moline is extensively used.

The metropolitan expectations of early days, before it was known what railroads would do for Chicago (by concentration) have hardly been realized by the Upper Mississippi river towns; yet it is a desirable region, possessing varied advantages and resources, and will yet become the classic ground of America.

The Hudson has now its day, and its beauty will not soon fade, or its fame be diminished; it will continue to be the gem of the east, but not of America; its location and limited extent will not admit of that. The Mississippi is our national river, and its shores will be our classic ground. Moreover, it will be anti-sectional ground, and its literature will help to extirpate those twin dragons of the past, sectionalism and fanaticism, and prepare the way for that charity and truth which is alone able to aid in the evangelization of the world.

Floating onward toward the west, the raft was making good time; but our friends had had no papers for some days, and were anxious to learn the political news. A steamer hove in sight, and as she passed close to them they hailed her and heard the news of the nomination of Lincoln for the Presidency by the convention of the Republican party at Chicago. At Muscatine they sent the skiff ashore and obtained the late papers, giving all that had transpired, and with the examination of these we will leave them for the night.

CHAPTER XIX.

THE next day the conversation very naturally turned upon the convention at Chicago, and its action, and both the friends agreed in expressing regret that Edward Bates, (the choice of Horace Greeley) had not been nominated instead of Lincoln.

"Few leaders, said the Doctor, "can resign into the hands of others political movements that have occupied their minds for years, and see them perfectly comprehended by men who have not shared that leadership. Seward and Greeley are political leaders, who have formed the Republican party, and who doubtless have a plan that is harmonious and practical for neutralizing the errors of southern propagandists (the extremists, and frequently the worst demagogues that we have in the south,) and they can the better do this, as they are not themselves considered the extremists of their party. Doubtless these men realize that time will make the slavery problem easier of solution, and Greeley saw in Bates an able, popular and conservative man, who, if elected, would allay rather than increase the excitement, and leave his party, at the end of his term, stronger than he found it—strong enough to carry the next election. Seward, doubtless, is ambitious, and wanted the nomination, and his election would not cause half the excitement that would that of Lincoln; for he is better known. Thousands of conservative, reflecting men of culture, in the south, have waited and watched the rise of the new party in the north, to see into whose hands its destinies would fall. They respect Bates, and would not greatly fear Seward, but they have no confidence in Lincoln, and, with all his plausibility, consider him the representative of Radicalism, and not a sound constitutional man."

"Has not his position been misrepresented?" said Sydenham.

"Perhaps it has," said the Doctor, "yet he has assumed the full panoply of the abolitionists, when he says that 'the country cannot exist part slave and part free, but must become all one, or all the other,' and that 'slavery must be placed in process of extinction.' This means revolution, and its effect is not removed by assurances that 'the existing institutions of the south are not to be disturbed.' They say they like Giddings and Lovejoy better, for they know where to find them."

"How will your radicals, the secessionists, like it?" said Sydenham.

"The worst of them will be well suited, for it will tend to make them and their position stronger and more popular," said the Doctor.

Here the friends sat some time in silence, each engaged in his own sad reflections.

"What do you think of the clause in their platform from the Declaration of Independence, declaring that all men are created free and equal?" enquired the Doctor.

"Why," said Sydenham, "as applied to the question to which alone it was intended to apply when written, justifying the colonies as against England, I think it correct and true, but as *now* sought to be applied by a political party, I consider it nothing but a piece of arrant demagoguism, and doubt whether three men in the convention believed it a month ago. Partisanship may yet make them claim its infallibility as it did make the other party claim the infallibility of the dogma of 'popular sovereignty.'"

"What a great cable of truth could be made of all these various strands of dogma, were as much pains taken to harmonize and blend them into one as there is to maintain their separate infallibility," said the Doctor.

"Parties rest their claims for office and political power upon the maintenance of their political dogmas," said Sydenham.

"We once had men who could rise to a higher plane than this," said the Doctor.

"Yes," said Sydenham, "Washington and a few of the great ones of the revolution could, and the result, under God, was the formation of the Federal Constitution, and a form of government that has commanded the admiration of the world."

"You are indeed correct," said the Doctor, "*there* was displayed the most conscientious discharge of duty, commanding intellect, and practical patriotism—patriotism large enough to extinguish sectionalism, and pure enough to restrain ambition. How lofty was the eulogium of Lord Brougham: *'While time lasts the measure of the progress of the nations of the world, in civil government and true liberty, will be indicated by their regard for the memory and example of Washington.'"

"And why," said Sydenham, "cannot we now have a 'National Constitutional Convention,' to settle all these vexed questions of 'free soil,' 'territorial rights,' the 'fugitive slave law,' and all other distracting questions that are

---

*Note.—This quotation is from memory, possibly not literal, but correct in substance.

beyond the power of Congress, the States, or the people. Such a convention is expressly provided for in the Constitution itself, is in harmony with the whole theory and structure of our government; with the opinions of Jefferson, the recommendations of Washington in his farewell address, with the christian religion, with sound political philosophy, and with plain common sense."

"That is all true; and yet that resort has been scarcely named by our statesmen, so-called," said the Doctor.

"I have heard it suggested that it would be well to hold such a convention once every twenty-five years," said the other.

"Perhaps it might," said the Doctor, "were we to begin now; but the spirit of innovation has been too strong, and it might have increased it; but were we to begin now, it would be different. Twenty-five years, now, is as much as fifty at the time of the adoption of the Federal Constitution, in hurrying us onward to error or truth, as the case may be. The people respect the prerogatives of the Federal Government, as conferred by the Constitution, and very properly are jealous of infringements upon the rights of the people or of the States. If the temper and disposition of the people is right, all necessary reforms can be carried through at all proper times by Constitutional Conventions, if only men are sent as delegates who will not sacrifice earth and heaven to their ambition. Should the fearful calamity of civil war now result, posterity will fix the responsibility of it upon the politicians, Congress and the party-leaders, as well as upon the extremists of both sections."

"Yet," said Sydenham, "we already have some men who talk lightly and glibly of war, as though it were sometimes a pure fountain of great good—a kind of healthful renovator."

"It is only a great evil, growing directly out of the depravity of human nature; yet, sometimes it becomes a hard necessity," said the Doctor.

"Were the principles of christianity adhered to by the nations professing it, wars would cease," said the other.

"Yes," said the Doctor, "terminate hypocrisy and you end wars."

"And were this done what vast armaments and boundless expense could be saved—enough to banish poverty and extirpate crime," replied Sydenham, with enthusiasm.

"You cannot banish poverty until you restrain avarice, said the Doctor, "and covetousness."

"No," said the raftsman, "and avarice is regarded in America as a cardinal virtue—especially successful avarice."

"That is due," said the Doctor, "in part to the seeming need in a new country of the concentrated power of wealth to develop its resources; but capital, though a good servant, becomes a bad master, and sometimes a tyrant and robber;'and, sheltered behind its legal prerogative, sucks out the life-blood of the embarrassed and the poor, and, so establishes and perpetuates misery and degradation."

"How firmly in the very foundation of and throughout the superstructure of the Bible, the adamantine principles of truth are laid, and how solid a foundation for a law-giver or legislator are the commandments of the decalogue," said Sydenham.

"Yes," said the Doctor, "and did the entire world accept them in completeness and sincerity, together with those added by our Savior, it could afford to dispense with an immense assortment of legal machinery."

"We would, however, need the Savior himself to administer it—the divine law," said Sydenham.

"Undoubtedly," replied the Doctor, "for I would sooner risk the lawyers than the priests in civil affairs."

"This goes to show the logical consistency of the doctrine of the millenium," said Sydenham, who now rose to make preparations for running the Lower Rapids, which they were now swiftly approaching.

CHAPTER XX.

THESE rapids, unimpeded as they were by any artificial structures, were not regarded with apprehension, as the water was high and the rocks were well covered. The rushing river bore them swiftly onward, and soon Keokuk, the "Gate City," at the foot of the rapids, was in sight. This fine little city, having the beautiful and rich Des Moines Valley at its back, as it were, and the Mississippi, with its channel unbroken by any more rapids, giving it a fine outlet to St. Louis and the south, is, and will always be, an important business point. Being on the west, or Iowa side, it does not at all interfere with its stately and beautiful Illinois sister, Quincy, which is seated upon the other side, some forty miles below. It is between these that the river, as we have said, makes its most westerly sweep or curve to the west. Just below Keokuk, at the mouth of the Des Moines, is the southwestern extremity of the State of Iowa. Then begins the State of Missouri, which we now have upon our right for full five hundred miles—a great State, indeed, and possessed of vast resources. Entering the great family of the United States at about the same period as her sister State, Illinois, she has not gained so great a population. Corn, the leading staple of Illinois, with its products, beef, pork, etc., etc., was wanted first; but the time is close at hand when *iron* must be produced from the ores of Missouri, on a vast scale, in quantities as yet scarce dreamed of; and then will come her day.

These two States, centrally located as they are, not with reference to territory merely, but to the position of navigable waters, the system of railroads, great cities, commercial centres, and the direction and concentration of population and wealth, must exercise a great influence in times to come upon the destinies of America. Both great in territorial extent, they are far greater in exhaustless resources, in minerals as well as in productive soil. In this last, as Illinois excels in her number of acres of rich land, so Missouri excels in greater diversity of valuable products. Illinois has unlimited stores of coal, Missouri of iron. Placed in juxtaposition, these staples will be combined, and an iron-working business be developed surpassing in magnitude anything yet seen in America. True national economy demands that this be done; and if the "manufacturer and the agriculturist" cannot be "placed side by side," they can and should be brought nearer together, and so the immense waste of transportation be diminished, and increase of wealth follow. The railroads, and all the vast interior demand for iron, should be supplied from western furnaces and mills; and, by this means, that commerce which increases wealth will flow through the land in strong and healthy pulsations. Agriculture and manufactures can thus be established on a basis more stable than has yet been known, and political health will be promoted.

No single nation in Europe, except Russia, has greater resources than these two States alone, of the great valley of the Mississippi. Well might De Tocqueville say: "The valley of the Mississippi is, upon the whole, the most magnificent dwelling-place prepared by God for man's abode." But, without a wise and just management of public affairs, and the maintenance of public virtue, these resources cannot be developed fully, and, if they were, it would not be for the general welfare. The quiet life upon the raft, with the tranquil enjoyment of the interesting natural scenery, adorned by farms, dwellings, fine towns and palatial residences, beautiful steamers in sight almost every hour, and occasional railway trains, made the friends disposed to contrast the scene with that presented to the first white explorers.

"These scenes are beautiful, and indicate increasing wealth, power and advancing civilization, do they not, Doctor?" said Sydenham, as they were floating quietly along in sight of Quincy.

"They do, indeed," said the Doctor, "and most interesting and beautiful to look upon; but you must not think me cynical if I say there is danger under this beautiful exterior."

"From what source?" enquired Sydenham.

"From the love of wealth, luxury and display," replied the Doctor.

"And yet, as human nature is constituted, we could not afford to abolish these," replied Sydenham; "and, if we 'appeal to history,' it would be hard to show that Sparta did as much for the world as Athens."

"We must learn from both," said the Doctor. "A christian nation should be able to improve upon both,—as we do in some things, though not in all. Little Sparta, by her virtue, temperance, valor, abnegation of wealth and luxury, self-denying patriotism and steadfast adherence to her institutions and laws, maintained her proud integrity for five hundred years, in glorious contrast with the despotism, luxury, corruption and crime of the eastern nations; and her example has been most useful to mankind,—a fine national illustration of many most solid virtues that never have been and never will be surpassed."

"And how of Athens?" enquired Sydenham.

"I do not think," replied the Doctor, "it could be correctly claimed that she encouraged a love of wealth, luxury, or display; but she did encourage and cherish a love of the beautiful, in art, literature and oratory. The power, originality and force of her genius never has been surpassed; the worn and broken ruins of her art are now our models, the remains of her literature our examples, and her philosophy the delight of all philosophers. In science, her footsteps were sure as far as she progressed, and the most eminent surgeons to-day read Hypocrates with pleasure and advantage. Yet with all this love of the beautiful, the perfect, the complete and the true, and of success in their attainment, avarice was looked upon, spoken of and recorded as a "disgusting vice," and luxury was discouraged as was the amassing of private wealth."

"Doubtless you are quite right," said Sydenham. "In these things, and in many others, we can and should learn much from them, not only in the things of which we have spoken, but in politics and in political dangers."

"Yes," said the Doctor, "any republic from now until the millenium can and should learn by the example of the ancient republics to guard against danger from ambitious demagogues, from violent partisanship, from sectional feuds and jealousies, from the love of military pomp and conquest, from too rapid acquisition of territory, from the secret intrigues of monarchies, and, greatest of all, from civil war."

"You make your enumeration of dangers longer than our present popular writers," said Sydenham. "They include everything in slavery."

"Yes," said the Doctor, "and therefore they fail to make the safest and truest application of the political lessons of the past: for all the ancient world practiced it, monarchies as well as republics. So, though theories may be put forward, no comparison or analysis can be made; yet it is clear that the institution, in a general sense—in the abstract —does not harmonize with the spirit of the age."

"Neither," said Sydenham, "do many other things. For instance: A measure is now pending in Congress of more practical importance, and that should be more beneficent in its results, than can well be estimated. I mean Curtis' Pacific Railroad bill,—a measure that has been agitated for more than twenty years, greatly needed for ten, and now ripe for consummation; and this is the most prominent bill before Congress,—daily under discussion; would quickly pass if the people urged it. And yet it attracts less attention from the press and the public than the prize-fight between Heenan and Sayers. Take the newspapers of the country to-day, and where you find one line urging this great work, you will find one hundred lines relating to an exhibition so brutal that, in the early days of the republic, it would have been looked upon only with disgust; and yet, you must admit that the press is a fair reflex of popular sentiment."

"True," said the Doctor, while he paced thoughtfully back and forth on the raft, "the spirit of the age, public opinion, or whatever you call it, while it should always be considered, is not always a safe thing to follow; and the frequent warnings of this in Holy Writ are undoubtedly founded in perfect wisdom. ' *Vox populi, vox Dei,*' will not always do. How often in the history of the human race has the very seed of truth, of right, of justice, liberty and law been preserved by one man, when the populace were, for the time being, given over to passionate or plausible error, to base evil, to cowardice, or to apathy, until waked at last by these faithful sentinels placed by God on the silent watch-tower of truth."

CHAPTER XXI.

WE will now pass over an interval of a number of days. Our raftsmen have passed the mouth of the Missouri; have passed St. Louis, thence on to Cairo and the mouth of the Ohio; then Kentucky lies on their left. The narrow point of this State that touches the Mississippi is soon passed, and then comes Tennessee. On the other side, the earthquake region about New Madrid is passed, and soon Missouri is left behind. And then comes the State of Arkansas. The summer travel from the south northward has now commenced, and the larger and finer class of steamboats are crowded with passengers.

We are now in a long stretch of the river above Memphis. The day is drawing toward a close, and the men on the raft, oppressed with the heat of the long summer day, and the increasing monotony and tedium of the voyage, are not in so pleasant a mood as when we last saw them. Seth Lane, the pilot, had been in a chronic state of ill-humor, excitement and apprehension, from the time of leaving St. Louis. The run through the " grave-yard," (as river men term that part of the river between St. Louis and the mouth of the Ohio) had been replete with difficulty and danger, from the numerous snags, which might easily be removed, and the river kept clear, if snag-boats were kept *regularly* instead of *spasmodically* in service by the government. A large steamer was in sight a short distance below, the black smoke from the tall chimneys pouring out in a dense cloud, indicating that the firemen were making unusual exertions, and that extraordinary materials of combustion were brought into use. Soon she passed them her paddle-wheels beating the water into billows, and her swell leaving the raft rocking in her wake. Her guards were crowded with passengers, and the after-part with ladies, who watched the raft with interest, and some waved their handkerchiefs. The pilot, in his surly mood, seemed to consider the gay crowds his personal enemies, and their waving of handkerchiefs only a taunt, and swore some round oaths as he took a fresh quid of tobacco.

"Hello," cried Sydenham, "there is another boat." And as he spoke another large first-class steamer was rounding the bend from below. The clouds of smoke pouring from her chimneys, and the motions on her forecastle deck, showing that they too were "shoving up the fires" to their utmost. Indeed, a barrel of turpentine (on freight) had been brought up from the hold, placed near the capstan, and the head burst in; and into this the firemen dipped the sticks of cottonwood: for it was *a race*, a Mississippi river *steamboat race*, and the excitement ran high, both among passengers, officers and crew; even the cabin-boys, and children among the passengers, entering into the spirit of it with all the enthusiasm ever elicited by any contest on the turf; indeed, far greater, for each and every person were direct participants. None can appreciate the intense excitement, except those who have participated, and these well know that the sense of danger is generally lost sight of, and so in this case, or such terrible combustibles as turpentine would not have been resorted to. And on this boat were our friends, the Barrona and Johnson families. Barrona was sitting on the after-guards, surrounded by his family and a large circle of traveling acquaintances—ladies and gentlemen—and there were many children on board, playing about, and talking of beating the other boat, which, it appeared, had passed them while they were "wooding." Barrona had taken no interest in the race, indeed, had deprecated it, alleging that there was fully enough danger without racing, and was talking with the ladies of the salubrious climate of Minnesota, when his son Pierre came back from the boiler deck.

"Now, father," said he, "we will beat the other boat, for the captain has got up a barrel of turpentine to make steam faster."

"Barrona rose at once in alarm, and started for the forward part of the boat to remonstrate with the captain against this recklessness. He had not gone half the length of the main cabin, when a sudden outcry, a sharp commotion, and the next instant flames climbing the forward part of the boat, warned him that the worst he feared had come. The men, in dipping wood into the open barrel and carrying it thence to the furnace doors, dripping it as it went, quickly made a pathway for the fire, and like a train of powder to a magazine, the flames from the glowing furnace in an instant followed it to the open barrel. An effort was then made to throw the barrel overboard, but in so doing it was upset upon the deck, and in an instant the fire fiend had complete control, and in less time than it takes to relate it, the whole forward end of the boat was enveloped in red and crackling flames. At once every soul on the doomed vessel realized that they were in the very jaws of death; wild, piercing shrieks rent the air; men of unflinching nerve and dauntless courage were paralyzed by the awful suddenness of the catastrophe. Women and children wildly clung to their husbands and fathers; men with blanched faces struggled desperately to tear out the stanchions and light woodwork to make floats; others ran to lower the yawl; others again to secure their baggage and effects; but all were compelled to crowd back toward the stern by the swift flames and suffocating smoke, which filled the cabin, for already the heat, almost as far back as the wheel-house, was oppressive beyond endurance. Isabella fell upon her knees, and raised her hands in prayer. Barrona and his son struggled to secure floats, but all realized that their chance of escape was more than desperate. Many men's hearts failed them utterly, and wild despair usurped the place of reason.

Meantime, high excitement reigned on the raft. Sydenham saw the first outburst of flame, when it leaped from the barrel; he saw the liquid flame spread over the forecastle deck, when the barrel was upset; he saw it leap upon and climb the cabins; he saw the attempt of the pilot to turn the boat to shore, which succeeded in changing her course, but in another instant the pilot had to flee from the pilot-house to avoid being burnt to death at his post. He saw all this, and his blood almost ceased its circulation, as the wild shrieks of despair rose on the summer air from the burning boat. Then one thought alone filled his mind, and prompted his whole soul to action—it was to save the people on the boat. One slender chance offered to do this, and he at once determined to improve it. The boat, turned from the channel, struck a sand-reef; her engines were still working, but the sand-reef held her. Sydenham determined to lay his raft alongside. Calling his men around him, he said:

"Men, there are hundreds who, in ten minutes, will be

drowned or burned to death; we must save them. I am willing to risk my raft and my life. Will you help me?"

All said, Yes; but when the order was given to lay her alongside, Seth Lane swore he was "not going to be drowned or burned to death to save anybody."

"You will not," said Sydenham, "for you can swim if the fire drives you from the raft."

"I know this river too well," said the pilot; "few men swim out who fall in the Mississippi."

"I will not talk," said Sydenham in a voice of thunder, "while women and children are being burned to death. Lay the raft alongside."

"I will not," said Lane with an oath.

"Then stand back," said Sydenham, seizing the sweep.

The pilot resisted. In an instant Sydenham felled him to the deck, and aided by the best of the men (for some sided with the pilot) the course of the raft was changed, and the swift current rapidly bore her toward the fiery mass.

Isabella had first seen the coming relief, and with glad cries called to her father. Then hundreds of imploring voices were piteously begging the raftsmen to save them. Those who had at first sided with the pilot now came gallantly forward and, under Sydenham's orders, began to wet down with buckets of water that side that would come in contact with the boat. The steamer lay with her bow pointing towards the shore; and, if the raft could be held at the stern, the rescue could be made with ease; but Sydenham knew that if, in the confusion, they failed to make fast to the stern, and were once carried by, then all hope was gone, for they could neither return nor check the raft. To lay her alongside, then, while by far the most dangerous course in respect to the safety of the raft and its crew, was the only course that offered any hope of saving more than a small portion of the whole number on the boat. The chance of saving nearly all the lives involved a fearful risk, and it was this that his men feared; but they quickly said, if he was willing to risk his raft and his life, they ought to be willing to risk their lives; and so, except the pilot, they aided with all the roused energy and force of brave, determined men. The Doctor worked with tremendous energy in spreading upon the raft the bedding dipped in water, and in wetting the now dry boards by throwing on water; but the time for this was too short to effect a great deal. The current bore them on so swiftly that soon the stern of the raft, which was next the bow of the boat, was so hot that men could scarcely stay on it, even by retreating to the further side.

Before she struck, Sydenham placed himself and most of his men nearest the crowd on the stern of the boat, and begged of them, in jumping on to the raft, not to crowd one another, and charging his men to aid the women and children first, and hurry them back to the other side, he set such an example on the raft, and Barrona on the boat, that, even in that fearful moment, something like system and order was established.

The boat was now one mass of fire, from her bow back four-fifths of her length, and, even at the extreme stern, the heat was so great that it was with difficulty some were restrained from plunging into the river. Before the raft touched, several men sprang from the boat towards her; and of these two or three fell into the water; and one was caught between the raft and the boat and crushed to death instantly. At the moment of contact the rush began, and, although every effort was made *by those seeking to save others* to prevent accident, many were hurt quite seriously by falling, and others from behind falling or jumping upon them. Directly after the raft struck, the chimneys fell with a loud crash, and one fell upon the raft. The boat also floated from the reef; and the fright caused by these two circumstances added greatly to the panic.

Barrona took his post near a stanchion at the stern, and had there gathered his own and Mrs. Johnson's family, and had made all join hands and press close together, to avoid being separated or pushed overboard by the surging crowd. When he felt the boat afloat he started and feared the boat and raft might part at once; another look, however, and he motioned them to stand still,—yet a moment or two, and the way was clear. With a quick motion to Sydenham, he seized Isabella by the hand and passed her to Sydenham, who bore her almost insensible form to the other side of the raft. His wife, Mrs. Johnson, and all the younger members of the two families, were quickly passed over the side and received into the strong arms of the raftsmen and Doctor Ross; and, just as boat and raft parted, Barrona, the last soul upon the boat, sprang on the raft.

And now a wild outcry was raised that the raft was on fire. And so it was, and had been from the time the chimney fell, and had been raging at one end of the raft while all were busy at the other. Sydenham and Barrona instantly consulted, (for such situations develop both confidence and perception of character) and, and at their suggestion, a line across the raft was formed, and each man or woman with a garment of some kind dipped in water was soon beating out the flames which were licking over the surface of the raft. This movement was so successful that confidence was soon restored, and men, women, and even children charged upon the flames from all sides with wet coats, shawls and petticoats. As soon as this work was well begun, Sydenham called all the raftsmen and steamboat-men to get them entirely clear of and away from the burning wreck. To do this poles were brought into requisition, and soon the men, with faces scorched to a blister, had the satisfaction of getting the raft entirely clear of the boat, and floating out of the range of that fierce heat.

Putting the sweeps, which were not greatly injured, in charge of his own crew, with the steamboat pilot to indicate the channel, Sydenham now superintended the complete extinguishment of the fire upon the raft. This was soon effected, and then all breathed free again, and could see how fearful had been their danger and how great their deliverance.

Within three minutes after the last had left the boat, most of the upper deck had fallen, and the stern, even to the rudder-post, was one mass of lurid fire. The light upper-works of the boat being of pine, and painted with oil paints, were now almost consumed; but the hull burned more slowly. Had the fire started in any ordinary way, the precautions constantly taken on these boats against such disaster, and the efficient discipline maintained, would have insured its immediate extinguishment; but the excitement engendered by the race led to the *careless use* of a dangerous combustible, and, after the upsetting of the barrel of burning turpentine, no human power could save the boat from quick destruction.* Order, discipline, courage, strength, or a self-sacrificing disposition, availed nothing then. Had every officer on the boat lain down his life, it would have availed nothing.

The raft was different, the top courses only being dry, and lying rather compactly together, and the whole surface

---

* About the year 1855, a steamer plying between St. Louis and Peoria was destroyed exactly in the way here narrated; but there was no rescue, and a large number of lives were lost. The catastrophe occurred a short distance above St. Louis.

except the little cabins being flat. Sydenham knew that the chances of subduing the fire were very good, and that if all would work that it was almost certain that it could be done with ease. The great danger was that the panic and confusion would prevent until too late; but the prompt action of Barrona and his family set an example that was immediately imitated by most of the two hundred passengers.

Isabella, on reviving after swallowing a little of the water hastily offered her by Sydenham, took her place by her father's side, and, tearing the skirt from her dress, dipped it in the river and sloshed the flames, after the fashion of the early settlers on the prairies of Illinois, "fighting fire" to protect their fences and crops when the prairies were on fire. Barrona recognized an old college friend in the Doctor, and, after a warm greeting and many expressions of gratitude, enquired for Sydenham, who, blackened, scorched and begrimed with smoke, fire and cinders, was now examining the extent of his losses.

The Doctor, who had seconded Sydenham with all his heart and soul, and had labored unceasingly in wetting down the raft before contact with the boat, then in getting passengers on board, and then in extinguishing the fire, told Barrona of the high excitement and mutiny on the raft, its prompt suppression by Sydenham, and the desperate and narrow chance by which they were enabled to come to their assistance at all. Barrona had to this point maintained his courage and comparative calmness, but he now gave way, and tears coursed down his cheeks. The Doctor led the way into the little lodging-room thus far occupied by himself and Sydenham, and there the strong men bowed their heads and returned thanks to God for this great deliverance.

"And now, my friend," said Barrona, "let us seek your noble friend, but for whom, under God, almost every soul on board that proud steamer would have perished. No words of mine can thank him enough, for he has saved what is far dearer to me than life."

Sydenham had just washed the smut and dirt from his blistered face, and was giving directions to his men about landing at the nearest town, which, the pilot of the steamboat told him, was about five miles below.

The Doctor approached. "My friend, Mr. Sydenham, of Minnesota; my friend, Mr. Barrona, of Louisiana."

"I have already become somewhat acquainted with Mr. Barrona," said Sydenham, smiling and extending his hand.

But Barrona took him in his arms and embraced him with emotion. "You," said he, "have done for me and mine what no words of mine can express. You have saved all of our lives, and at the peril of your own; and if Henry Barrona, now or ever, can do aught to repay this obligation, command him."

"I did no more than my duty," said Sydenham, "and, without the aid of many others, among them the Doctor and yourself, could have effected nothing; but I am most thankful to God that you have all been saved, and that we are now here on this raft in safety."

"But come," said Barrona, "let me present you at once to my family and friends, that they too may thank you."

"I thank you for your kind offer," said Sydenham, "but you see I am in no plight to go among ladies, and no raftsman could face so many at once as I see in that crowd forward."

"Tut, tut," said Barrona, "no wife or daughter of mine would heed such trifles in such a case, or I would disown them."

But Sydenham pleaded his duties on the raft, and begged to be excused until after they landed. The Doctor went with Barrona, and was introduced to Mrs. Barrona, Mrs. Johnson, and the families of both. The ladies enquired anxiously for Sydenham, and expressed their gratitude in most earnest terms; and numbers of gentlemen went to seek and thank him, while others proposed more substantial rewards; and soon a committee was formed, and a subscription of over five thousand dollars was made up, as a compensation to Sydenham for losses and a reward for his efforts. The paper was then handed to Barrona, who glanced it over, and then placed his name on it for five thousand dollars. Several other subscriptions were made; and a number of ladies subscribed liberally. The gentlemen then waited upon Sydenham, and told him what they had done, and that the money should be collected and paid to his order at any bank he might name in St. Louis, Memphis, or New Orleans.

Sydenham was taken by surprise. He had indeed heard that a subscription was being taken up to pay him for the lumber that was burned, and make good his losses; and he had been pleased at this; but, always self-reliant and proud, he revolted from the idea of receiving the bounty of these wealthy strangers, no matter what the circumstances. He thanked the committee for what they had done, but told them that his losses would not exceed one thousand dollars, and more than that he would not accept, and even that he had not expected and did not ask.

The committee urged that it was all right for him to accept the whole, and that they would not feel satisfied if he did not do so; but Sydenham assured them he had only done his duty as a man, and that he did not think it right or proper to accept anything more than compensation for actual loss, and positively would not. Finding Sydenham decided, the committee retired to consult with Barrona and the Doctor, who were surrounded by a group of ladies, among whom were Isabella and her mother. The committee stated that Sydenham would not accept. Barrona felt mortified at this, and Isabella blushed. Taking the Doctor to one side, the two talked for some time. Returning to the group, he took the committee to a remote corner of the raft, and said to them:

"Gentlemen, we have all made a mistake. This is a very different man; and if we would even repay him his losses, we must wait a day or two. His whole trip is broken up, and his raft in a condition that he cannot go down on the coast as he intended, but will have to sell his lumber at Memphis. Perhaps the sum he named will cover only the actual value of the lumber burned, and if he is obliged to sell on a bad market he may lose in that way, also. Let us retain the paper as it is, until we find out his full loss; and this he can and must accept."

As most of the passengers designed stopping a day or two in Memphis to recruit, this proposition met with general favor.

The captain of the steamboat, who had been considerably burned and injured, and had been carried to Sydenham's berth, now sent for him, and suggested that instead of landing at the little town which they were now very near, that they go on to Memphis, where every accommodation could be had. This he gladly assented to if the passengers would agree to it; and they, finding they could reach the city in about three hours, or by eleven o'clock at night, and that the trip would be entirely safe, were nearly all in favor of it. It was now dark, but there was a brilliant starlight; the signal lights had been put out, and the sweeps were in charge of the best men on the raft, aided by some of the steamboat crew, while the steamboat pilots stood by to indicate the channel, they being at home with every bend, island and chute, as a man with his door-yard, and by night as well as by day, familiar with the channel, and knowing where are the snags and where the deep and where the shoal water. Few men realize what it is to be a good Mississippi river pilot, and fewer still can make one. Of course the raft-pilots, are not expected to know the river as thoroughly as the steamboat pilots, nor is it necessary.

Seth Lane had not offered to touch the sweeps, nor to assist in any way; nor would Sydenham have permitted him to do so, since the affray when his resistance and refusal to obey orders had almost cost the lives of the people on the steamboat.

The cooking caboose with its contents had been burned, so that no supper could be had until they reached Memphis. Seeing that all needed arrangements had been made, Sydenham went forward with the Doctor, and was presented by Barrona to his family, and that of Mrs. Johnson; and here, by the starlight, standing upon the charred and blackened boards, floating onward upon the great river, we will leave them to converse upon the terrible events of the day, and other topics that would be suggested by so peculiar and unusual a situation as that in which they now found themselves placed.

CHAPTER XXII.

WE have said that Isabella was the first one on the burning boat to discover the approaching raft with aid and the hope of life; of rescue from a watery grave, or a death of horror. With her mind strung to its utmost tension, and every faculty of mind and soul aroused, nothing on the approaching raft escaped her eye, and, as it floated near, and Sydenham stood forward, his form dilated by excitement, and gave his orders, snatching them all from the very jaws of the raging flames, she felt a torrent of wild emotions that she had never known before. Tears rolled down her cheeks; and when her father handed her almost fainting form to the arms of this gallant stranger, she could not speak nor utter one word. When he gave her water, she could only raise it to her burning lips, and when he left her, and her father summoned her to aid in extinguishing the fire on the raft, all her energies seemed to revive at once, and no woman upon the raft rendered such efficient service; and now, although the fire was over, and she stood beside her father, mother, relatives and friends, and knew that all were safe, her mind had not become tranquil. She heard but little that passed around her; and, leaning her head upon her mother's breast, she wept.

"Why, my dear child," said her mother, " we are now safe, and all are rejoicing, and yet you weep; surely you do not grieve for the loss of your jewels and clothing, when God has spared us all alive and unharmed."

"No, no, dear mother, those things are nothing; I care not for them, and we have been blessed and saved, and I rejoice and praise my Maker; and yet my heart is sad."

Seating her upon a rude seat that had been hastily made out of some boards from the part where the fire had not reached, her mother bathed her throbbing temples with water from the river, and tenderly wiped her face with her handkerchief. Anxious inquiries were now made by some of the passengers for the party who had gone off in the yawl; and fears were expressed that they might have met with some accident, as it was overloaded, and filled with men, the most of whom knew nothing of managing a boat. It was at this juncture that Barrona introduced Sydenham to the ladies of his family, as related at the close of the last chapter. By the dim starlight all traces of weeping were concealed, and Isabella felt as though she were in her father's house.

At first the all-absorbing topic with the whole circle was the startling events of the day. Save the man crushed between the raft and the boat, no lives were known to be lost; though, as the boat's books and papers were all lost, this could not be certain, especially as it was not known, positively, who and how many were in the yawl, and whether they were safe. Of those who were injured, all would recover, it was thought; and as there were several physicians among the passengers, all had had all the attendance that could be given until they reached the city. These subjects disposed of, other topics came up, and the conversation went on, not as between strangers, but as between friends, reposing confidence in each other. All barriers of formality and reserve were broken down, and Barrona, his wife, Mrs. Johnson, the Doctor, and Sydenham conversed with that warm and kind cordiality, the peculiar charm of which can only exist where perfect mutual esteem, confidence and sincere regard are felt. At first, Isabella took very little part in the conversation, her mother and aunt leading, but Sydenham was far too gallant a man to long neglect any lady; and Isabella expressed a desire to see the way in which the unwieldy mass was controlled, and kept clear of the eddies and snags her father had pointed out to her from the guards of the boat. Sydenham offered his arm, and they walked off to where the pilots and raftsmen guided the raft by means of the sweeps. They then walked to the remote and unoccupied part of the raft, and watched the dark and silent shores, covered with primeval forests, and laved by the rushing river.

"Do you like to be upon the river, Miss Barrona?" enquired Sydenham.

"Yes," said Isabella, "though I was born upon the banks of the river, and have passed nearly all my life there, yet I never tire of it; and when father took me to the splendid Hudson, although I enjoyed it very greatly, yet I was glad to get back home to the banks of the old river."

"Have you ever seen the Upper Mississippi?" enquired Sydenham.

"No, I have not," replied Isabella; "and I had anticipated so much pleasure from seeing it; but oh, how little I thought of the horrors of the past day;" and she covered her face with her hands, and again the unbidden tears coursed down her cheeks.

"But this is, I hope, all over now," said Sydenham, "and soon you will be safe in Memphis."

"Oh, pardon my weakness," said Isabella, "it is not all for myself, but for father, mother, brother, sister, aunt, cousins, all these, and friends and fellow-travelers, placed in a moment between a horrible death by fire and drowning in this dark, rapid river, (and the poor girl shuddered and sobbed) and from this dreadful fate you saved us all, at the peril of your own life. Oh! what if you had not been in sight, or had not come to our aid; how can we thank you enough?"

"I thank a kind Providence for the opportunity," said Sydenham, "but forget it all, Miss Barrona; I did nothing but simply my duty, and, had I been in peril, your noble father would have done as much for me," said Sydenham.

"Indeed, I know he would do all he could," said Isabella, proud of the terms in which Sydenham spoke of her beloved father; "and so," she said with enthusiasm, "would I, if I could."

"Indeed you did," said Sydenham, "and noble service rendered in extinguishing the fire almost under our feet."

Isabella laughed. "I must have made a singular appearance," she said, "but I suppose you gentlemen were too busily engaged to criticise me."

"Our criticism could not have been otherwise than favorable," said he.

A steamer from below was now in sight, and they paused to look at her as she approached. Steaming onward, in the plenitude of her power, it was a striking contrast, and the quick mind of Isabella at once remarked it.

"How proud and grand a thing is that steamer," she said; "and yet," she quickly added, "this raft is safer, and, humble, as they think it, it saved us when they could not," she said, with a wave of her hand toward the steamer.

"Yes," said Sydenham, "humility is sometimes safer than pride."

"Is it not always?" said Isabella.

"Certainly humility before God, and before ourselves, is always right," replied Sydenham.

"Then," said Isabella, "you do not believe in too much humility before men."

"Not before some, I do not," said Sydenham decidedly.

Isabella smiled. "Tell me," said she, fixing her dark and piercing eyes upon his, "why is it that some of your northern politicians accuse us of the south of being proud? are we any more so than you of the north?"

"Indeed, Miss Barrona," replied Sydenham, "that is a question I cannot answer. I only know that there is quite too much crimination and recrimination among the politicians and newspaper men, of a sectional character, for the good of the nation; and as to pride, I do not see how a few parallels of latitude can make much real difference in human nature, at least with a people of one blood and lineage."

"No," said Isabella, "and as to pride, how absurd most of it is—I mean nearly all pride."

"Yes," said Sydenham, "the love of the true and right is far better; but you spoke of loving this grand old river of your country. I sympathize with you in this, and hereafter shall love it more than ever."

"And so will I," said Isabella, "in spite of its terrors."

The lights of Memphis were now in sight, and preparations were made for landing. Barrona took occasion to explain to Sydenham and the Doctor, that he should remain in Memphis a few days, and would expect them both at his hotel, on the morrow, or at their earliest convenience, when he had something to propose to them. To this invitation the two friends replied that they would be most happy to call, either the next day or the day after.

The bustle of preparation now took up the attention of all, and in half an hour the raft was moored in front of the city, and all the passengers and crew from the burned steamer had left for the hotels, save only the two watchmen left on the raft for the night.

CHAPTER XXIII.

THE next morning Memphis was full of excitement at the news (brought by the survivors themselves) of the terrible disaster that had overtaken the splendid steamer Comet. The hotels were full of the passengers, and the all-absorbing topic throughout the city was the terrible affair and the numerous incidents connected with it. The captain of the boat was severely censured for permitting the careless use of turpentine; but, as he himself was severely injured, and a heavy loser pecuniarily, being owner of one-half the boat, on which there was but little insurance, whiich it was thought might not be paid, there was a disposition generally manifested to overlook his fault, and extend to him sympathy in his misfortunes. This was all the more manifested as it became known that but one life was lost—the man crushed between the raft and the boat. Many were seriously burned but none dangerously. The escape of the people without great loss of life was a standing marvel, especially with the river men, and more particularly the officers and crew of the Comet. And nearly all agreed that the rescue was wisely and bravely managed. A few, of course, insisted that it was all luck; that it might and should have been managed better, etc., etc. The passengers having lost all their clothing, except what they had on, tailors and dressmakers were in great demand, and some of the ladies (among whom was Isabella) were obliged to keep their rooms until new garments could be provided. As Barrona had his money and drafts on his person, he saved all; but many were not so fortunate. Sydenham was busily engaged among lumber dealers, in selling his lumber, for which he found a favorable market. Dr. Ross, finding that his expected voyage was now ended at Memphis, was undecided what he would do; but, having made all his business arrangements so that he could be absent from home until the beginning of November, he was free to choose as his wishes might prompt. He had already taken up his quarters at the same hotel with Barrona, removing his baggage from the raft.

In the afternoon he and Barrona called to see Sydenham, but finding him busily engaged in landing his lumber, they exacted a promise that he would come to their hotel in the evening, after the day's work was done. Accordingly, in the evening, Sydenham laid aside his raftsman's dress, and attired himself in a proper suit for an evening visit, and, calling at the hotel, sent up his name to the rooms occupied by his friends. But Barrona had placed his son in the hotel office to wait for his friend; and, before the man could start with his message, Pierre Barrona came forward and conducted Sydenham at once to the family parlor, where were assembled all the members of both the Johnson and Barrona families, except Isabella, by all of whom he was most warmly greeted, with enquiries as to whether or no he had suffered from the over-exertion of the day previous. To all these kind expressions Sydenham replied that he had not suffered otherwise than feeling some slight soreness in his limbs and muscles; and all complained of some soreness, to some extent, from over-exertion, and a slight cold, from exposure to the night air, after being so heated and so fearfully excited. None, however, had suffered from the fire except Barrona himself, whose neck, hands and face were badly scorched.

Soon Isabella was announced; and Sydenham, dazzled at the beauteous and resplendent being who now, clad in simple attire, stood before him, rose with diffidence and took her extended hand. In the wild excitement of the rescue, he had too much thought of saving to pause to admire; and, in the evening conversation on the raft, it was too dark to more than see the outlines of her form and features, and, although he had been charmed and delighted, he little dreamed of the vision of grace, goodness and beauty that now stood before him.

" Mr. Sydenham," said Isabella, as she extended her hand, " I hope you have not suffered personal injury in your efforts to save our lives."

" Not the least, Miss Barrona," said Sydenham. " On the contrary, I feel most happy that the issue was so successful, and that a kind Providence rendered it possible for me to aid you."

Tears suffused the large, dark eyes of Isabella, and for a moment she could not speak. At a sign from her father, however, she mastered her emotion and said:

" Mr. Sydenham, to-morrow morning high mass is to be held in the Catholic cathedral, to return thanks for our deliverance; and although we suppose you are not a Catholic, yet we would all most cordially invite, and, indeed, urge you to accompany us, and participate as your feelings may dictate."

" I thank you for this kind invitation, Miss Barrona," said Sydenham, gravely and respectfully, " and accept it; for I can see no reason why Catholics and Protestants, worshiping the same God, should always refuse to do it together: certainly they are, or should be, one in Christ."

" You are quite right," said Barrona, " but you know

the walls of bigotry that have been built on both sides, and which some say cannot and must not be overleaped; but I think and act otherwise."

"I rejoice," said Sydenham, turning to Barrona, "that you hold such liberal sentiments. For myself, although no Catholic, and believing that errors have crept into that great church, as into others, yet I have always respected it, and have not believed it to be the monster many zealous Protestants honestly think it to be."

"I am a moderate and conservative Catholic," said Barrona, "and moderate and conservative Catholics and Protestants, it seems to me, need not be far apart, although the priests of both too often tell us differently."

"Yes," said Sydenham, "and some of them are continually rebuilding the walls and embattling them; whereas, we would level them, or, at least build them no higher between the followers of the crucified Redeemer."

Dr. Ross was now announced; and the conversation turned upon other topics. An hour—two hours sped away so swiftly that neither Sydenham nor the Doctor realized that it could be so late, until a glance at his watch by the latter showed that it was time to retire. Bidding Barrona and the ladies good-night, Sydenham and the Doctor withdrew, but paused a moment at the room of the latter, who gently rallied his friend thus, (after first closing the door of his room, and glancing around to see that there were no eavesdroppers:)

"Well, old friend, I must say that, for a raftsman, you have proved yourself a great ladies' man; indeed, I was astonished, and did not know but we would have another conflagration, so brightly sparkled the eyes of the young lady; and yours, though not of the fiery kind, usually were not far behind. I did not know but the curtains of the window near which you sat would take fire from the electric flashes."

"Indeed," replied Sydenham, "to own the truth, I never passed so pleasant an evening in my life; but I did not intend to show it. Tell me truly, Doctor," he added, gravely, " as a friend, was my behavior in any way amiss, or in the slightest degree improper?"

"Not a bit," said the Doctor, gaily, "you only acted as ingenuous young men of your age are apt to do when they fall madly in love; and she," he added, in a lower tone, "seemed quite determined to make the plunge, also, without stopping to look."

"For shame, Doctor," said Sydenham; "say what you will of me, but do not utter one word in even slight disparagement of such a being as this."

"Ah," thought the Doctor, "I have, then, a true diagnosis of the case."

"Not for worlds, my dear fellow," replied he. "I never saw but one lady whom I more admired; and she was not a thousand miles away."

"Ah," replied Sydenham, "now I think of it, I recollect seeing a medical friend of mine, of mature years, paying high court, recently, to the matronly beauty of a certain lovely widow."

"Ah, my boy," said the Doctor, deprecatingly, "don't say a word, for you hit me in a tender spot."

"What! so soon?" queried Sydenham, maliciously,— "leaping headlong without first looking: you at least are old enough to know better."

"Oh," said the Doctor, holding up his hands imploringly, "murder will out; murder will out; but not another word let us utter on this subject to-night--not another word," and, so saying, the friends shook hands and bade each other good-night, Sydenham going to his raft and to bed, but not to sleep. The bright vision of Isabella's beauty was bright before him, and sleep he could not. He thought of the Doctor's words almost in anger; but then he knew that the Doctor was his friend; and he rejoiced that he had a friend with him who knew something more of him than those whom he had so recently met.

CHAPTER XXIV.

THE next morning at nine o'clock, the Barrona and Johnson families, accompanied by Sydenham and Ross, with a number of passengers from the burned steamer, proceeded to the cathedral, which was soon filled with the escaped passengers and crew of the boat, and citizens of Memphis. A large number of ladies were present The occasion was a most solemn and interesting one; and to Sydenham the services were new and unusual. As the beautiful and solemn music pealed through the arches of the lofty building, his mind and soul seemed to absorb and fill with the glorious influences of religion, and he saw only the worship of his Maker and Savior, and his soul seemed lifted above all the petty distinctions of sect or dogma. The solemn service ended, Sydenham escorted Isabella, and the party returned to the hotel.

Here Sydenham left them and made his way to his raft, where for two days he was constantly engaged in superintending the landing, assorting and tallying of the lumber. This done the sale of the different lots was consummated, the account of the burned lumber made up and settled for by the treasurer of the committee at the same price he received for the other, which was all Sydenham would receive.

The men on the raft were each presented with one hundred dollars besides compensation for articles of clothing lost by them. In this distribution Sydenham was willing that Seth Lane should share; but not so the men on the raft, or the donors, who insisted that these rewards were tokens of merit, and marks of esteem to the men, in which he ought not to share; for, in addition to mutiny, he had rendered no aid, even in the most dreadful moment. Sydenham would have perhaps taken this same view, but the man had come to him, after the landing at Memphis, confessed his fault and asked his pardon; and this had taken away all his anger and disposition to punish him any farther in any way. But the pilot felt deeply his disgrace, and as soon as Sydenham had settled with him and paid him his wages, he started for home on the first boat bound up. The other men remained; and, after taking Sydenham's advice to remit most of their money to St. Paul, went about the city, enjoying themselves in their own way, and lionized by the Memphis boys greatly. But after two or three days spent in this way, the more staid portion induced the others to start with them for home, which they did, in high spirits, and accompanied to the boat by a large number of their new friends, among whom were some of the crew of the Comet. Sydenham bade his men good-bye on the boat, receiving from each expressions of esteem and good-will. Barrona and the Doctor also came down to bid them good-bye, and Isabella had sent to each one a handsome present by the hand of Burton, whom the Doctor had brought to her for that purpose. His business concluded, Sydenham took up his quarters at the hotel, his room adjoining the Doctor's.

Meantime Barrona had made all the necessary arrangements for the families to go on to Minnesota; and now tendered to both Sydenham and Ross a warm and pressing invitation to accompany them. Sydenham accepted this invitation, of course, for he was going at about the same time, and he knew that they were aware of this, and to decline or make excuses would seem odd, or as if designed. But the Doctor was embarrassed; he wanted to accept, but it seemed to him awkward to do so.

"You see," said he to Sydenham, as the friends sat in the quiet of the evening twilight, by the open window, in Sydenham's room, "for me to turn right about with you and go back to Minnesota, from whence I have just come, when I live down here, would seem unusual, and even absurd; and how do I know but they might have only invited me out of politeness, because I was with you."

"You flatter me," said Sydenham; "but I will not be flattered. How do I know but the high favor you think I enjoy is due entirely to my friend Doctor Ross, and to his former acquaintance."

"You have no grounds for thinking so," replied the Doctor, "and every ground for thinking otherwise. True, Barrona and I were old college friends; but we had not met for years, and my introduction of you to him amounted to nothing under such circumstances. You had been instrumental in saving their lives—that introduced you; and afterwards these high-souled people knew intuitively what and who you was."

Suddenly the memory of Grey Eagle's dying words flashed upon Sydenham; greatly agitated, he started to his feet and paced the room. The Doctor looked at him with surprise; he trod the room with such a pace that the floor quivered and vibrated; his whole form dilated with excitement, hands clenched, and teeth set. The Doctor rose from his seat in alarm.

"Sydenham," said he, "what is the matter? are you ill or mad?"

"Neither, my friend," said Sydenham, pausing and

lying his hand upon his shoulder. "Pardon my behavior. You recollect the dying chief, Grey Eagle. He died on this same raft on which we were permitted to save the lives of all these people, and of this bright being with whom you say I am madly in love. He uttered some singular words of prophesy about my future wife, and how I would win her; and now your words of friendly encouragement brought this to my mind, and fixed the connection, and wonderful indeed if it should be fulfilled, and this glorious girl be mine,—but that is wild, and I must not let so sweet a delusion possess me."

The Doctor paused a moment in thought. He recalled the words of Grey Eagle: "She comes to his arms out of the fire and is his wife." Instantly the excitement of the Doctor knew no bounds. He manifested every emotion of wonder, joy and fear, and seemed unable to control himself. Seeing, however, that his friend was not disposed to converse, he betook himself to his own room, and there meditated in silence upon what seemed so great and wonderful a mystery.

As for Sydenham, his mind was in too great a tumult to think, and leaving his room, he walked out alone into the streets of the city. Passing along out of the gay and crowded thoroughfare, he entered a fine colonnade of beautiful shade-trees. Here, near the lofty porch of a public building, he was accosted by a woman—one of that degraded and unfortunate class who minister to the sinful pleasures of others. Giving her some words of kind advice, and handing her money to relieve her wants, he passed on. Reaching the bluff back of the city, he paused for some moments, and looked over the lights of the city to the dark line of river beyond; and his mind turned upon all the strange events of the last few days, and then upon the aged Indian chief, and the strange chance by which he was able to rescue and relieve him, to soothe his dying hour, and to give his remains christian burial. Then before the voyage was ended, comes this fearful calamity, and out of this the woman who now filled all his thoughts. Would the prediction be fulfillled, or was it but a delusion and a snare? Could it be possible that he was to be so blest, or was he to drink the cup of a bitter disappointment? He rose and slowly walked back to his hotel, and to his room; and here, in silent vigils and in prayer he passed the night.

CHAPTER XXV.

THE morning broke gloriously, the crimson and yellow light streaming far up above the horizon. Sydenham watched it until the great orb of day was above the horizon's verge. Leaving his room, he descended to the street and walked out. Passing through the silent streets, he wended his way to the river-bank, and sat down to muse. The great river rolling on its tireless course seemed to him a type of life, ever changing, and yet unchanging in its onward course towards the great gulf and the greater sea, like to the tide of time rolling onward toward eternity.

Musing in listless reverie, he sat for some time, until at length roused by the arrival of a large upward-bound steamer from New Orleans. The lines were made fast, the gangway planks run out, and soon the passengers came ashore. The omnibus for the hotel drew up near him, and a gentleman of fine appearance, and most elegantly dressed in the hight of fashion, approached and enquired of the hotel runner for the Barrona family; if they were stopping at the hotel. Being answered in the affirmative, he entered and the carriage drove off. A sudden pang entered the heart of Sydenham. He felt that this elegant and handsome stranger was and must be the suitor of Isabella, and all the pangs of love, jealousy and despair tugged at his heart-strings. He hastily rose and went to the hotel and to his room, and, after making his toilet, descended with his friend to the

breakfast room. They had not been long seated when in
came the Barronas, and Isabella on the arm of the handsome stranger. They took their seats near, and the
stranger was introduced to the friends as Mr. De Vere, of
Baton Rouge. Sydenham rose and extended his hand,
and received his thanks and congratulations, (rather pat-
ronizingly given) as the rescuer of his friends, &c. A
great effort was now made by De Vere and Sydenham
to be polite to each other, but the freedom and ease of the
little circle was gone. Naturally, the conversation turned
on the escape, in which Sydenham did not wish to say
much, and then on affairs in Louisiana, and then on politics, in which De Vere maintained the extreme secession
view. At length the breakfast ended, and Sydenham
retired to his room. Here the Doctor soon joined him,
and said it had been proposed by him to Mrs. Johnson
that they (the whole party) have a ride to-day in the
country; and urged him to at once see Isabella and invite her to accompany him. Sydenham did so; and she
accepted his invitation before De Vere was aware what
was going on, and greatly to his chagrin. Finding that
the family were going, he invited Amelia Johnson to
accept his escort in a single carriage, but that young lady
had already accepted the invitation of her cousin Pierre.
Mortified at this second failure, he was a little soothed by
Mrs. Barrona, who invited him to a seat in the family
carriage, which her husband had then gone to engage.
This invitation he accepted, greatly to that lady's satisfaction, who considered the arrangement very proper and
right all round, and who made no disguise of her very
high esteem for Sydenham, in the course of conversation
during the day. Barrona, also, although a friend of De
Vere, took occasion to express, in unequivocal language,

his gratitude to Sydenham, and his high regard for him, in terms that he intended should effectually suppress any further patronizing air from De Vere toward him.

De Vere felt keenly the gentle rebuke, but most deeply was he pained when, half an hour later, the carriages were announced, and Isabella, arrayed for the occasion, entered the parlor, and, taking the arm of Sydenham, descended to the street. He had, indeed, aspired to the hand of Isabella, and well might expect success. Handsome, wealthy, talented, holding an eminent social and political position in his native State, (Louisiana) few ladies, indeed, but would be delighted with his attentions, and ready to accept his hand. But neither Isabella nor her parents were to be influenced by these things too greatly, and although she had respected, and even admired him, yet she never had loved him; and this he felt more than ever before, as he saw the look she bestowed upon Sydenham, as she, radiant and happy, took his proffered arm.

It was arranged that the family carriage, being driven by a driver acquainted with the roads, should lead; then followed the Doctor and Mrs. Johnson, then Sydenham and Isabella, and then Amelia Johnson and Pierre Barrona. A gentle shower, the night before, had laid the dust, and the fresh morning air of early summer was loaded with fragrance, and enlivened by the songs of birds. As they ascended the bluff, the beautiful little city lay below them, and from the summit they had a commanding view of the city, river and valley.

Few cities can boast a more lovely site than Memphis; and there are, upon the whole, few more beautiful towns. From the river back to the summit of the bluff there is a gradual rise, securing perfect drainage and a most beautiful effect, as viewed from the river, the bluffs, or from the city itself. The party halted for some time to enjoy the beautiful panorama. While they looked, a stately steamer rounded out from the landing place, and steamed down the river, glittering upon its waters in the sunlight like a floating palace.

Pursuing their way, they drove out into the country a few miles, and returning by another road, reached the hotel about eleven o'clock, except Sydenham and Isabella, she having expressed a wish to enjoy the view of the city and river again, from the same point, and they accordingly returned the way they went, and, driving slowly, were half an hour later in reaching the hotel. The ladies withdrew to their rooms on returning, and the gentlemen to theirs; but all met again at the dinner-table; and here Barrona proposed starting again for Minnesota, on the boat expected from New Orleans that evening—a very fine and very safe boat. And now the Doctor found himself in a position that he must decide whether to go or not. Barrona, Mrs. Barrona and Sydenham urged him to go with them, as did Isabella; but the Doctor hesitated. Finally Mrs. Johnson remarked:

"Doctor Ross, indeed I hope you will decide to go back with us; it will be so pleasant."

To this the Doctor at once replied: "Thank you, Mrs. Johnson, I will go."

This settled, the Doctor's embarrassment was now over, but De Vere found himself in an awkward position. He had come up, on hearing of the accident, intending to accompany the family, not doubting that his company would be every way acceptable; but he found the situation quite different from what he had expected, and, to use a homely but expressive phrase, he was a kind of "fifth wheel to a wagon." As for Barrona and his wife, the friendship and intimacy between them and De Vere and his family disposed them to the utmost kindness and courtesy; yet they could not conceive how his presence during the trip, as one of the party, could, under the circumstances, add to its harmonious enjoyment. The Spanish mother knew well the characteristics of her race, and saw clearly the unchanging impulse of her child, and knew that nothing from any other source would change the current which neither father nor mother had tried to check. De Vere rose hastily from the table and went out. As the party rose from the table, Sydenham whispered a word in Barrona's ear, and, after seeing the ladies to the parlor, the two friends went to Sydenham's room. Closing the door, and handing Barrona a chair, Sydenham seated himself.

"Mr. Barrona," said he, "since chance threw us together, I need not say how great a pleasure to me has been the society of your family and yourself, nor how grateful I am for the courtesy and the marks of friendship and confidence you have shown me."

"My dear friend," said Barrona, seeing his friend's emotion, "say not a word; it is me that should be grateful."

Sydenham continued: "You will, I fear, think me abrupt, and possibly, presumptuous, when I say that my own peace of mind demands that, before we start north, I must ask you one question."

"Say on," said Barrona.

"Would you permit me to address your daughter with a view of marriage, and win her if I could?"

"I will," said Barrona, " and if you win her I will win an honorable and high-souled man for a son-in-law."

Sydenham's emotion almost overcame him. Until the last twenty-four hours, he had hardly dared to allow himself even to *think* of such supreme happiness as calling this lovely girl his wife; and now, that her father had so nobly given his consent, and that he had learned from her own lips that De Vere was to her only a friend, hope like the full-orbed sun roused his passion to an impetuous torrent. But, checking himself instantly, he said:

"But, Mr. Barrona, remember, I am poor and have no wealthy family connections, nor have I had the advantages of a thorough education, or of social intercourse with the gifted and learned."

"As to your circumstances," replied Barrona, "I think you told me that the proceeds of your raft would pay your debts and leave you some ready money, and that you had some property, and that you had supported yourself from a child, and had struggled, unaided, in the world for all you had won."

"I did," said Sydenham; "but yet, I would not be able to place your daughter in the position I would wish to, should I be so fortunate as to win her."

"My daughter comes of a line of women who, if necessary, are willing to accept even poverty, with those they love. Isabella could not be won by wealth or position; so, my boy, if you win her, remember, it is for yourself, alone."

Sydenham was deeply affected. He pressed the hand of Barrona, and that gentleman withdrew. An hour passed, and Sydenham heard a knock at his door. Opening it, De Vere entered. Offering his hand to Sydenham, he said:

"You are, allow me to say, a most fortunate man."

"How so, Mr. De Vere?" said Sydenham.

"Why," said De Vere, "I came here this morning with high hopes of winning a most lovely woman, and thought that, after an acquaintance of years, my chances were good; but I find you, my dear fellow, hold all the cards—father, mother, the lady herself, probably, and all her family and relations. But," added De Vere, gravely, "I learn that you are a brave man, a man of honor, a christian and a gentleman; and I resign all claims to the man who saved her life, and offer you my friendship and best wishes for your success and happiness, and assure you I am not going to die of a broken heart, or of jealousy."

Sydenham grasped his hand with deep emotion, and thanked him for his generous, manly and magnanimous conduct; and calling his friend, Doctor Ross, the three friends enjoyed a half-hour of pleasant, social intercourse, and then left the hotel, to make their last arrangements for the trip. De Vere, however, was not going until the next boat, and then to Louisville, "where," (said he gaily, as they parted) "I am going to make love to a lady even more beautiful and accomplished, and every way as interesting as the good, true and charming Isabella Barrona."

"I wish you success and happiness," said Sydenham; "but can I too succeed, I would not exchange her for all the women in the world, and the world itself added."

De Vere paused and looked at him intently a moment.

"It is all right," said he; "but I am not that kind of a man, and can bear a disappointment of this kind better than you can. But I again tell you that in this affair you are the favorite of fortune; for not often do men like you succeed in these matters, and," he added after a moment's thought, "let me advise you to marry her quick, while the current is so strong in your favor, or else some adverse tide may set in, and even you fail at last."

The young men pressed each other's hands. "Thank you, a thousand times, thank you," said Sydenham, "and may God bless you and yours forever."

CHAPTER XXVI.

JUST as the sun was setting, the splendid steamer Constellation, Captain Scott, Master, steamed away from the Memphis landing with the whole party on board. Isabella and Sydenham sat near each other, upon the after-guards, engaged in conversation; while, at a little distance, Barrona and the Doctor were reading some late papers, the other members of the families being in the cabin or upon the upper or hurricane deck. The conversation between the pair, after the city of Memphis was left behind, had turned upon books.

"Mr. Sydenham," said Isabella, "you have read Shakspeare; now tell me which female character of his you like the best."

"The purest diamond in the whole casket is, I think, Miranda, in the play of Tempest," replied Sydenham. "And which do you admire the most, Miss Barrona?"

"Indeed, Mr. Sydenham," replied Isabella, timidly, "I am no critic, and have never read Tempest, but I have heard my father say that he thought the best female characters in the Bible (the old Testament) and in Shakspeare harmonized; that Ruth and Miranda were alike; and then he would kiss my mother and call her his Ruth sometimes, and sometimes Miranda, but her name is Isabella, like mine."

"Your mother was from Spain, I believe," said Sydenham.

"Yes," said Isabella, "and there my father married her

and brought her to Louisiana, his native State, and where his father died; and there I was born, and there we have all lived very happily; but my father says he fears now that great troubles may come upon the whole country. He says the people's minds are so inflamed by evil speech, evil writing and falsehood, that the north and the south hate each other, and he fears war may break out, and he fears the prosperity, liberty and virtue of the country may be destroyed, or greatly injured, besides the killing of thousands and thousands of men."

"Indeed, it is too dreadful to think of," said Sydenham, "and as foolish as wicked."

"Oh, Mr. Sydenham," said Isabella, while the tears dimmed her lustrous eyes, and her bosom heaved, "you would n't fight in such a war, would you?"

"I think not," said Sydenham, "for it seems to me the duty of a true patriot to oppose civil war under almost any circumstances."

"Mr. Sydenham, will you point out the place where the Comet burned, and where you saved us from perishing miserably," said Isabella.

"With pleasure, Miss Barrona; but it will be after dark when we pass there; yet I can show you about the place, and the wreck may be visible."

"Oh, Isabella," cried Mary Barrona, "come up on the hurricane deck; it is so pleasant."

"Will you not go up, Miss Barrona?" said Sydenham; "there is a fine promenade there."

Isabella rose. "With pleasure, Mr. Sydenham; but I will go and get a light shawl, for the night air will be cool soon."

Sydenham stepped to his state-room and, exchanging his light summer coat for one of cloth, met Isabella in the ladies' cabin, and, offering her his arm, escorted her to the upper deck, where numbers were promenading in the cool evening air. It was now twilight, but the landscape, softened by the approaching gloom of night, offered its own peculiar beauty at that hour, as the noble steamer held steadily on her way. As they walked forward, the dark eyes of Isabella were turned up the river.

Forward of the tall chimneys, near the bell, Barrona and Doctor Ross stood in conversation with the captain of the boat, and surrounded by some of the younger members of the party and several other passengers. As Sydenham and Isabella approached, Barrona introduced them both to Captain Scott, who was an old acquaintance of his.

"I am happy to see you, Captain Sydenham," said he, "and to thank you for saving the life of my brother, who was captain of the ill-fated Comet, and of his passengers and crew. A lucky thing, indeed, that you happened along just at that time; and even then, with ninety-nine men out of a hundred in charge of that raft, there would not have been one-quarter of them saved."

"I saw," said Sydenham, "that it would be quite impossible to save more than a very few, except by laying the raft alongside; and this course looked so very dangerous that it was almost defeated by an attempted mutiny on the raft. Then, fear and panic on the boat came near ruining everything; but our friend here (your brother being disabled,) held it in check; and then this gentle lady," turning to Isabella, "by her devoted efforts to stay the flames on the raft, set a noble example that was quickly followed, and we were soon safe from that last danger."

Isabella blushed deeply and cast down her eyes, and her hand, which rested on Sydenham's arm, was observed by the bronzed captain to involuntarily tighten its grasp.

Tears came into the veteran's eyes. He raised his hat respectfully to Isabella, bowed, and said in a low tone, " May God bless you both."

The pair resumed their promenade in silence, while the captain and Barrona sat down near the bell. Soon the boat landed at a wood-yard, and, by the time she had finished " wooding," the moon was up, and shed its pale light over forest and river. As they passed the scene of the disaster, the pilot pointed out the wreck, having learned its exact position from a brother pilot in New Orleans, who had noted it as he passed down.

The promenaders had now deserted the deck, except only Sydenham and Isabella, who walked aft and looked upon the charred and blackened wreck, upon a sand-bar quite near the track of their boat. As they passed near it, Isabella could not contain her feelings, and the horror of that awful hour seemed to fill her mind.

"O surely it was a heaven-sent chance that brought you to our aid," she said, with deep emotion. " Think of father, mother, brother, sister, aunt, cousins, and all, perishing in a moment, and their bodies given to the fishes or the flames. I can never forget it,—never, never."

Sydenham gently soothed her; and soon the swift steamer had left the blackened wreck behind. The pale moon rode serenely through the azure heavens, as the lovers sat in that beautiful night, on the steamer's deck, and yielded themselves to the serene and sublime influences of the hour. No word was spoken for some minutes.

" Isabella," said Sydenham, in low and gentle accents — for so she had told him he might call her—" Heaven forbid that I should claim gratitude from any one for a simple performance of duty, which God made successful; but I feel that I must tell you, even *now*, that my heart is yours; that I love you with all my soul. Tell me, dearest Isabella, may I hope for a return, or will you reject me?"

Isabella spoke not, but laid her hand in his. He pressed her to his bosom, and kissed her again and again. She leaned her head on his breast, and wept tears of joy. For she knew from her mother, to whom she had confessed her love, that her father would not refuse her hand to Sydenham: and there and then their vows were plighted.

CHAPTER XXVII.

THE next morning Sydenham told his friend, Doctor Ross, that which the good Doctor rejoiced greatly to hear—his engagement to Miss Barrona.

"My friend," said the Doctor, "I thought you looked taller than usual, this morning; and indeed you do."

"And so I should," said Sydenham, "if my feelings influence my stature; for I feel happier, aye, and greater, than if I had come in possession of an empire."

"But remember," said the Doctor, "that saying of the eastern sage when asked for an inscription to put upon a ring, that should moderate the transports of joy in the hour of success and happiness, and soothe the pain of grief in the moment of adversity and disaster: 'And this too shall pass away.'"

"Excellent," said Sydenham, "but my life has been one of toil and self-denial; and now let me enjoy while I may, for trouble will come soon enough, doubtless. This is the time to be happy; and I am determined not to go in search of dark care, but hide from him, rather, for a time."

"You are quite right," said the Doctor, quickly. "I would do so myself, if I was situated as you are; *and I wish I was,*" he added, with great emphasis.

"I think you stand high in the lady's estimation," said Sydenham, "and as the successful usually assume to give advice, allow me to suggest a homely adage: 'Make hay while the sun shines.'"

"Confound your adages," said the Doctor. "If I should

attempt a rapid movement and get floored, you could find half a dozen old saws about the folly of too great haste."

"Pardon me, my friend, said Sydenham, seeing that the other was not disposed to levity, "I will not and do not intend to commit the folly of seriously offering advice; but you know you have my best wishes, as has all the world; and I would impart to all a share of my own happiness, for I have too much; and you may exercise the prerogative of a friend in my behalf by restraining me, for I feel as though I could walk right out through the thin air, and climb the clouds."

"You really frighten me," said the Doctor, "and I have no straight-jacket, nor is there any means of taking care of the insane here."

"I wish," said Sydenham, "that you would hasten to the same point in this delightful pilgrimage to which I have reached; and then you, being afflicted with the same glorious insanity, could, as a physician, prescribe a change of air; and we would go back to one of those beautiful little lakes in Minnesota, away from the unappreciative or envious crowd, where there was only woods and rocks and the four pilgrims, devotees at Love's shrine."

"Really," said the Doctor, "I always thought you a temperate man; but here you have been drinking champagne before breakfast."

"Champagne, indeed!" said Sydenham. "It was the nectar of the gods, and taken hours ago; but now I am going to be practical. Let us go down and see the ladies to breakfast; and do not you utter one word of all this, for it might give grave offense,—not, I hope, to Isabella, but to others."

Isabella had risen early, and, calling her cousin, Amelia Johnson, the two had walked, arm in arm, for some time on the after-guards of the boat. Both families were now in the ladies' cabin, and, directly after the two friends entered, the polite steward announced breakfast, and Sydenham escorted Isabella, and the Doctor Mrs. Johnson, to the sumptuous table. The long and spacious cabin of the steamer presented quite a vista of elegant comfort.

The western river steamers are, upon the whole, the most pleasant and desirable mode of traveling yet inaugurated. Free from the plague of sea-sickness; free from the intolerable smell of bilge-water and oil, that all-pervading nuisance on ocean steamers; free from the dust of railway trains; large, airy, with ample space for exercise, both in the cabins and on deck, shady and quiet nooks on guards, etc., with ample opportunities for social intercourse, or for privacy, with excellent fare in great abundance and variety, and cleanliness and order everywhere, it is not probable that any more delightful, safe or healthful means of travel can be devised. Then one is free from the annoyance of showing tickets, feeing waiters, making bargains, etc. The traveler goes on board, engages his neat little state-room, pays his fare, and is treated with courtesy and attention. As to safety, accidents, of course, do sometimes happen; but they are of rare occurrence. Good order, discipline and efficiency are the rule, both among officers and crew; and courtesy and pleasant social intercourse, combined with attention to one's own business, is the etiquette of the cabins. These rivers, draining the whole vast interior of the continent, are used for travel by thousands of every class; and an immense variety of character is here met with. Men from the north, the south, the east and the west; from the Pacific to the Atlantic oceans, from the British Possessions to Mexico, and from almost every country in Europe. A certain class of somewhat narrow-minded and hypercritical writers have given very unfavorable and unjust impressions in regard to life upon these boats; and few, indeed, have been found to pay a just tribute to the high ability, courage, generous manhood and honor of western boatmen, or to appreciate the difficulty and hardships of their vocation, as well as its peculiar temptations. Not all these critics would be able to fill even subordinate stations, or to acquit themselves creditably in this kind of a life.

Captain Scott sat at the head of the table, and, after those from the ladies' cabin were seated, the breakfast bell was rung, and the long table was soon filled. Long and leisurely meals are not the style here, consequently there is less conversation; but, as there is abundant opportunity for conversation all the rest of the time, this is not objectionable. If the passengers can all be seated at the first table, after they have risen, it is spread anew for the officers of the boat; and here freedom, jests and repartee prevail. Then, after this, the cooks, cabin boys, waiters and chambermaids are served. The deck crew are served below, and the mode of doing this might be improved.

CHAPTER XXVIII.

ON board the Constellation were gathered a large number of passengers from almost all parts of the Union, of various character, vocation and station in life; representing, in a good degree, the various phases of American life and character, diverse in thought and in interests, having all shades of political and religious opinions, and, upon the whole, not a bad type of the nation. Of course, at the time of which we write, politics was the all-absorbing thought and topic of discussion. The great Democratic convention at Charleston had been held, and had ended disastrously, in the dismemberment of the Democratic party. Few reflecting men but had great misgivings of the future; but as there are not a great number of this class, the temper of the disputes and discussions did not differ greatly from those preceding other Presidential elections, only that there were more radicals or extremists, and extremes were further apart—indeed, directly opposite. Although south of Mason and Dixon's line, all shades of opinion were well represented and ably maintained, and, through the example of a few leading, high-toned gentlemen, courtesy and toleration were the rule, so that, although passionate and angry discussion ran high, yet personalities were generally avoided. Occasionally the hydrophobia of ultra slavery, propagandism or its opposite extreme, would be developed; but as the number of those afflicted in this way was but small, and as the radical element dominated, they were kept under such restraint as to preserve the peace on board the boat, and so prevent the spread of either contagion. On board the boat, also, were several gentlemen who had attended the Democratic convention at Charleston, S. C., as delegates, and many sad things, illustrative of the dangerous elements entering into American politics, were shown to have been in existence there, in the course of a long, calm and analytical examination of the subject, entered into directly after breakfast, and continued during the day, in the quiet seclusion of the after-guards, by a small circle consisting of Barrona, Ross, Sydenham, and four or five other gentlemen of various sections, (including some returned delegates) who were not in any way interested in violent agitation, but were sincerely interested in the peace and well-being of the country. The result of their analysis of the subject was agreement upon these points:

1. That there existed two parties, one in each section, who were inflexible in their purposes, unprincipled and unscrupulous in the choice of means, and determined to have their own way; and these parties, though really small in numbers, were incorporated into and led the great bodies to which they belonged; and, as neither could succeed in their objects so long as the people were united, so it was their interest and aim to dis-unite the people, and encourage sectionalism and sectional hate, and the blind fury of the populace.

2. That money from some source in large sums was at Charleston, for the purpose of corrupting the delegates; that this was well known, and that the very air seemed tainted with bribery, as never before known in America; and it ought to be known whence came this money for purposes of corruption in such vast sums.

3. That European statesmanship and diplomacy do

not repose upon the basis of christianity, but upon that of self-interest, or national aggrandizement, and do not and dare not dispense with vast armaments for their maintenance.

4. That their secret fear of the spread of American institutions is well known, and their intrigues to be dreaded and guarded against.

5. That it is absurd and grossly improper, every way, that the oldest, largest and most powerful political party in America should have at the head of its organization the known and accredited agent of the house of Rothschild.

6. That while permanent servitude *as an abstract principle of right* is fallacious, the real good of the country, or of any portion of the people of the country, does not require any violent measures, or the dissemination of any revolutionary principles.

7. That men possessed of inordinate ambition, and violent, brawling demagogues, and all other demagogues, are and always have been the bane of republics, and have been and will be of this republic.

8. That as the last resort of political differences in this favored land, civil war should not even be thought of, nor secession, nor coercion, but rather a NATIONAL CONSTITUTIONAL CONVENTION, assembled in accordance with the constitution itself, and with the opinions and plan of the founders and makers (under God) of the government, above States and Congresses, and the fogs of partisanship; above the vile malaria of sectionalism, and above the diabolical *perversion* of christianity, patriotism and truth; and in the pure and bright light of true patriotism, christianity and truth, and, in a spirit of concession and kind regard, each for the other, a spirit of true humanity and justice, discarding public ap-

plause, disregarding the fear or favor of any party, class, or section, and all the enticing dreams of ambition; emulating the patriotism of Sparta, and following the divine precepts of christianity; refreshing, restoring and perpetuating democratic republican institutions in all their purity, vigor and excellence; conserving and protecting all the interests of all the people, of all the States, without antagonism toward other nations, but with good will toward them, yet that good will guarded by vigilance and shielded by power; extending, also, its duties to shelter beneath its ample breadth, and protect, in strict justice to ourselves and them, the red and black species of the human race, and all other types over whom our laws are extended, or with whom we are brought in contact, and who cannot become a part of the body politic by reason of essential differences that can only be abrogated by Omnipotence.

9. That such a convention we believe possible and practicable; and even if it cannot come up to this standard, it would still be the only proper resort; and should the country drift on into the breakers of secession and civil war, it can be THE ONLY ISSUE THEREFROM that would preserve the principles of such a government as ours inviolate, and protect the people from the manifold dangers of corruption, violence and misgovernment.

After the gentlemen had discussed these points and embodied them in writing, it was suggested that the passengers, officers and crew of the boat be gathered in the cabin, the propositions read to them, and the sense of the meeting be taken upon them; and it was agreed that, made up, as it would be, of people of all classes and sections, it would represent, in a good degree, the real mind, heart and feeling of the people upon these questions,— the sentiments of the heart of the west. But the day was now so far advanced that it was thought best to defer this meeting until the next day, especially as many violent partisans would certainly oppose, from opposite points; and to Barrona, Sydenham, and, indeed, all the party, it was something more than mere amusement,—they wished to know whether or not these sentiments would accord with the popular heart. That they would please politicians could not be expected; for both and all parties might construe something therein contained into an attack upon them, and so would oppose and deride the resolutions, and claim that they did not meet the points at issue, etc., etc. But the party broke up with the understanding that the voters on board the boat should be appealed to, the next morning; and then Sydenham, Barrona and the Doctor sought the ladies' cabin in time to escort the ladies out to supper.

Isabella's serene beauty seemed illuminated, and, as Sydenham gazed upon her, he felt a sorrow at his heart at the thought that she could ever fade and die. And then, with mighty force and power, came into his soul the glorious hope of the christian, and, after the supper was over, they walked again upon the upper deck, until the stars came out, and then sat down alone, and gazed into the azure heavens, and talked of the brightness and glory of the future world, and of the blessed Savior, and their hope in him in the future, and gratitude and love to God in the present existence. And so the sweet hours sped away until ten o'clock; when, with a kiss, the lovers parted for the night, and then, each to their room, to devotions, and then to bed.

CHAPTER XXIX.

OF course the engagement of Isabella and Sydenham was made known to Mrs. Johnson, and the immediate friends of the family, after it had been assented to and ratified by her parents, which was done the next morning, but in a very quiet way, to avoid the publicity that otherwise would be given to it upon the crowded steamer. But both Sydenham and his friend, Doctor Ross, were treated as and understood to be of their traveling party, and usually escorted the ladies to the table; and so upon this morning.

As yet the dark war-cloud did not overshadow the land, and, although there had been some warm political discussions on board the noble steamer, yet genial and kindly influences had always prevailed. This morning Captain Scott seemed in a remarkably good humor, and, after the passengers were seated at the breakfast table, remarked to Barrona that he understood they were going to have a Union meeting on board, and, on being answered that they were, remarked gallantly that he hoped they would secure the influence and attendance of the ladies; that, if they were for the Union, the men would be, of course.

"They have got them all right," said Pierre Barrona, roguishly; "and I think we may consider the Union safe."

Isabella blushed at this sally of her brother, and Mrs. Johnson looked reprovingly at her nephew; but Barrona replied gravely that he feared "if the men were wrong, the ladies would be found generally in full sympathy with their husbands, fathers, brothers and lovers; and, therefore, if the country were in danger of civil commotion, the ladies would be found taking sides like the men. And men," added he, "who refuse to take sides will, I fear, be misjudged, persecuted and despised."

"But," said the captain, "the ladies, from their natures, must be averse and opposed to war, should anything so terrible as that ever occur, which may God forbid."

"I do not know about that," said Barrona. "The love of war seems to be innate, and its 'pomp and circumstance' are as captivating to the one sex as to the other."

"O, no, father," said Isabella; "I feel sure that is not, could not be the case with me, for I should think too much of the sufferings of the unfortunate victims, of the innocent and poor, who suffer while war exists and after it ends."

"You may well say, 'after it ends,'" said Doctor Ross, "for the war ceases not with the fighting. It begins then; and war suffering follows in the train of what is called glory."

"May heaven defend us from both the suffering and the glory," said Mrs. Barrona.

After breakfast was over and the tables were cleared, the passengers began to assemble; and the officers and crew who were not on duty were invited to join them. The meeting was called to order in due form, and a gentleman from New York City was called to the chair.

Barrona then made a few remarks explaining the object of the meeting; and the resolutions were then duly read and offered by a fine-looking portly gentleman from Illinois, De Main, who had assisted in framing them, and who had also been a delegate at Charleston, and had borne testimony of the corrupt money influence brought to bear there.

The chairman then rose and, claiming the privilege of a few remarks, objected strongly to the fifth resolution, on the ground that it reflected on the patriotism and integrity of an eminent gentleman of his city, who was his friend, and whose character he considered assailed, and thereupon he would ask the gentleman to strike out that resolution.

Dr. Ross here rose and said:

"I can assure the gentleman it was not intended to assail his friend, for with us *persons* are *nothing* and *principles everything;* and that the principle is sound and true, I think the gentleman himself must admit; and his friend, if, as he is said to be, a man of high and pure patriotism and unblemished integrity, must also, if candid, admit the correctness of the principle, and, if the application of it reflects upon him, retire at once from a position he should never have accepted; for I repeat in the language of the resolution, 'That it is absurd and grossly improper that the oldest, largest and most powerful political party in America should have at the head of its organization the known and accredited agent of the house of Rothschild.'"

A murmur of approval passed through the assemblage; and the chairman rose and said:

"Gentlemen, as you have honored me with the position of chairman, of course it is not proper that I should debate, and I will only say that if the resolution was not intended to be personal, I withdraw all opposition to it; and, indeed, as a rule of action in a general sense, I *heartily concur*, and am obliged to the gentleman for the suggestion, for, when I reflect upon it, I am *astonished that such a thing was ever done.*"

Barrona. "For one, I thank the gentleman most sincerely for his acquiescence and his candor, and earnestly hope that perfect candor and disregard of the trammels of party may, in this little assemblage of fellow-travelers, for once prevail; for, even the memory of it may, in future, days be pleasant."

A gentleman from Ohio here rose and said:

"Mr. Chairman, with all proper respect for the gentleman who prepared these resolutions, which in the main I approve, I must say that I think in the second resolution the great party to which I belong is reflected upon, and, if they belong to the same party, as I am told most of them do, I think it strange that they should give such a weapon into the hands of the enemy as a charge that corruption (through the use of money for purposes of bribery) existed in the convention at Charleston. I, for one, do not believe it, and even if it were true, cannot see what good can come of publishing it to the world."

Sydenham. "Mr. Chairman, I object, in toto, to some of the gentleman's views. He speaks of 'the great party to which he *belongs*,' and of the party to which we *belong*. Now, with all due respect for the gentleman, I object to that expression, at least for myself; for, while I am willing to *act* with that party which I think right, or nearest right, I am not willing to *belong* to any party whatever; and this thing, of a man *owing fealty to a party*, is, it seems to me, an error; and it is also an evil that should be abated,—banished forever. The question strikes me very differently, and I would, first of all, wish to know if it is *true* (and we have positive evidence that it is); secondly, if true, it is *a public danger that menaces the whole country*, and may effect any and all parties. Then, too, if it is kept concealed, it is far more dangerous in every sense than if known; for, if known, a remedy may be applied. But I am ready to admit that, in the application of this remedy, some judgment should be used; and, of course, in times of high political excitement, opposing parties are too ready to seize every opportunity to injure an opponent, without regard to truth, or the real interests of the country, or to healthy political action for the benefit of all. But this little meeting is not designed to be a political party meeting, conducted by politicians seeking office, but a meeting of citizens, seeking only the right, the true, and the healthy transaction of the public business of the country, for the country's good; and before such a meeting, all parties may be properly called to an account; and, if gross corruption exists in any party, it must be extirpated as soon as practicable, or that party will be ruined, and, of course, by its ruin the opposition would come into power. It is not necessary, always, to publish a wrong to the world, but it is always necessary, and a duty, to right it if it can be righted. That corruption, in some form, will creep into any party is expected, and the party that covers, conceals and protects it will (or ought to) lose power, while the one that is known to extirpate it will not be the loser by so doing. We do not propose to give the weapons for this extirpation to the enemy to overthrow us, but to *use them ourselves, that he may not overthrow us*, for the party will be stronger after being purged of this villainy than before."

The correctness of this position being conceded they were about to vote upon the resolutions, when a northern radical took the floor, and harangued the meeting with mighty voice and violent gesticulation for an hour, opposing the resolutions   He was followed by his anti-type, a radical fire-eating secessionist, for another hour, who, like his predecessor, succeeded in inflaming the passions of his auditory to a high pitch. He, too, opposed the resolutions. When he finished, Barrona spoke for twenty minutes. The resolutions were then read again, by request, and adopted, amid great applause, by nine-tenths of the meeting, which then adjourned, just as the steward came in to arrange the tables for dinner. But before the meeting dispersed, Capt. Scott proposed three cheers for a National Constitutional Convention, which were given with an energy that drowned the noise of the engines, and made the echoes of the forest ring again.

CHAPTER XXX.

THE boat was now nearing St. Louis, which city the captain expected to reach by 4 o'clock P. M. Meantime, after dinner, political discussion went on in groups all over the boat; and conservative sentiments dominated. But yet, as few or none could look into the future and foresee the gathering tempest of civil war, so few seemed to realize the full measure of the propriety and necessity of a National Constitutional Convention — the ark of the covenant. The so-called statesmen—leaders of political parties—had not presented this measure, nor urged it, so only a few analytical thinkers saw in it the cap-stone of the great structure of free constitutional government, reared in America, under the Providence of God, by the men of the Revolution.

Nor could it be expected that it should be otherwise; for the ship of state had floated so grandly in the ordinary channel, that only those who saw an extraordinary crisis could be expected to look for this extraordinary channel, laid down in the original charts by men whose voices are no longer heard on earth.*

---

* Washington, in his Farewell Address, evidently alludes to this resort; and Jefferson says substantially that "foreigners have an idea that the States are subordinate to the Federal Government." This, he says, " is an error; that they are not subordinate but co-ordinate branches of one great whole; that usually the mutual interest and good sense of the people of the States and the nation will be sufficient to preserve the harmony of government, but that, *when these restraining influences are not sufficient,* then a convention of all the States must be held." And, in the convention that formed the constitution, there was a party

Moreover, the long rule of partisanship and sectionalism, each operating in different ways, like counter currents wearing away an island in the Mississippi, had reduced the amount of true national sentiment and kindly regard by the people of different States for the other, and that community of interests upon which it reposed, the people were made to believe, did not exist; and so the true sentiment of nationality was reduced to so low a level that the country was ready for civil war, when pride, fanaticism and ambition joined, and a combination of unfortunate circumstances favored.

But these views were not held by the little circle of gentlemen referred to. They were full of anxiety, but hope prevailed. Although they believed the so-called Republican party contained the germ of mighty evils, like Pandora's box, and which might be strewed, far and wide, making a wreck of much that was good, and jeopardizing all, yet they believed, also, that it contained some good elements, and they hoped that these would prevail.

Barrona was sanguine that if the Republican party elected their candidate, the leading men of all parties would form a patriotic union, and that a National Constitutional Convention would result; whereas, if either the Democratic or Union (Bell and Everett) parties were successful, secession would have no force or strength to effect any harm; that it would practically be a "dead cock in the pit," and all would be well.

---

who thought this bond of Union (mutual interest, good will, etc.) was not sufficient; and it was proposed to give the Federal Government the power of the sword. This *was refused;* but especial careful and far-seeing provision was made for the convocation of all the States in a National Constitutional Convention. Evidence might be multiplied; but almost every intelligent, unbiassed man, then and now, would be a witness that it is in harmony with the whole spirit and structure of our government.

So, in this way, care was banished, and the approaching union of his daughter with the man of her heart was unclouded by aught to mar its happiness; and, yielding to the solicitation of Sydenham, it had been arranged that the nuptials should take place at St. Paul, within a week after their arrival there.

The full and generous soul of Isabella reflected itself upon all with whom she was associated, and brightened the social circle of the cabin; and, observing the hard and scanty fare of the deck passengers, and thoughtful for their comfort, she had quietly made arrangements with the steward (first obtaining Captain Scott's consent) to send them a bountiful meal, each day, from the cabin; and the deck crew were also the recipients of luxuries through her, for the gallant old veteran, Captain Scott, and her father, would deny her nothing.

As for Sydenham, he had sometimes thought, during the trip, that he must be under a spell of enchantment,— in enchanted land, his happiness was so supreme, in the presence of his affianced and the circle of such sincere and appreciative friends, so new a thing to him. The religious element, always strong in him, seemed now fairly at floodtide, and his soul seemed exalted into a new and glorious existence. If dark and scowling glances of envy or suspicion were directed toward him, he never saw them: he saw only the trusting, confiding countenances of friends, and Isabella; and, in the quiet of his little room, his soul went out to God in grateful prayer.

And now the trip of the Constellation is about to end, and the city of St. Louis is in sight. Stretching along the great river for many miles, and back upon the hills and slopes of Missouri, she sits a queen—a "River Queen." Chicago may claim justly to be the queen of the lakes, and boast her Briarean arms of her railways, but St. Louis has the rivers for her portion, and in this regard her domain cannot be surpassed upon this earth. As the steamer approached the city, the passengers came out upon the guards, and looked upon the panorama of life and commerce, outspread upon their left, and upon the river above them. Long lines of steamers of various classes lined the levee, from every part of the great valley of the western continent—from the Rocky Mountains to the Alleghanies, and from St. Paul to New Orleans. And besides the great main arteries of this vast river system of the continent, the secondary tributaries were also represented. Steamers from the Illinois, the Tennessee, the Cumberland, the Red, the Arkansas, and many other minor tributaries, lay side by side with those from the Lower and Upper Mississippi, the Missouri and Ohio rivers. And now the boat is landed, and the press and bustle of metropolis is heard and felt; the staging is adjusted, and the passengers walk ashore. And now follow four or five days of city-life, and, of course, preparations for that coming event which is to be celebrated at St. Paul. And here we will close the chapter, and in no way obtrude upon the secrets of the toilet; and we will ask our lady readers to accompany our heroine, in imagination, in these various details of shopping, &c., to which our pen can in no way do justice.

CHAPTER XXXI.

AFTER spending one day in visiting objects of interest in St. Louis, in company with the Barrona family, Sydenham was to take the evening packet for Rock Island, where he had some business to transact, intending to rejoin them on the steamer upon which they would ascend the Upper Mississippi when she would arrive at that point.

Mrs. Johnson had advised against so early a marriage of Isabella and Sydenham, and insisted that it would be more proper to defer it until the winter, and have it take place at home in Louisiana. But Sydenham's ardent solicitation, that it be not deferred, to which, finally, Isabella timidly assented, at last overcame all opposition. And now that they were about to part for only a few days, and be separated only by a few hundred miles, the open-souled girl could in no way disguise her feelings of apprehension for his safety, and told her mother, to whom she confided all her thoughts, that she was glad she had refused to delay their marriage, as her aunt wished.

The Doctor now found himself in a new position; for, as Barrona had business in St. Louis that took up about all of his time, the Doctor felt bound to escort the ladies on all their shopping and other excursions, at least the first ones. But the gallant Doctor entered into this new line of business with great zeal, and with a full sense of the responsibility resting upon him; and the lovely widow smiled archly as she witnessed his heroic efforts to do all that could possibly be expected, and to meet every requirement. On one evening the whole party attended the theater, and witnessed the charming play of the Lady of Lyons, greatly to the delight of Isabella and the younger members of the family, though, indeed, it was about equally enjoyed by all. Before the last day, the Doctor paid a visit to a friend, a few miles out on the "Iron Mountain Railroad," and so was absent from the party during a portion of their stay in St. Louis. But he returned on Saturday evening, and accompanied them to public worship on the Sabbath. And then, on Monday at four o'clock, P. M., the party took passage for St. Paul on the fine steamer Northern Belle. Before the boat started, Barrona telegraphed to Sydenham, according to previous arrangement, and Isabella, looking on as he was writing the despatch in the cabin, asked for the pencil, and wrote her name under her father's, asking him if he would please see that the operator repeated both names.

"Why, my child, this is nonsense," said Barrona, "and will cause remark."

"Dear father," said Isabella, "indulge me in this, for, as I could not write him, and have never sent him any message, what could be more proper than that I should send him one *first* by the lightning's flash. It was through the fire that we first met and became acquainted, and what could be more appropriate."

Her father smiled and gave her his consent; but her mother looked gravely on and said:

"I hope, my dear daughter, it will not prove to be an omen of evil, for certainly it is unusual."

"Dear mother," said Isabella, "I know nothing of omens; but it cannot be wrong to use the telegraph for such messages any more than for business."

But in the years that followed, when their heart-strings were wrung by swift, unutterable woe, when civil war spread its dark pall over the land, the circumstance was recalled, but the recollection caused no pain, but rather soothed grief; for it was not the outgrowth of folly, or vanity, but of love and truth; and, if it prefigured destiny, the warning was kindly and salutary.

And now the beautiful steamer for the north backed out from the levee, and the party went upon the hurricane deck to have the better view of the upper part of the city. The steamer held her course just outside the long line of boats that lined the city front; and it was highly interesting to observe these various boats (the representatives of a vast interior commerce) and the people upon them. St. Louis is built almost entirely of brick, and a very good view of it may be had from the river, along which it extends much farther than it does back from the river. At present, intercourse with the east side is kept up by means of ferry boats; but doubtles, a bridge, for the passage of railway trains, will soon be finished, although the work will be one of great magnitude and difficulty. The city is soon left behind, but the turbid flood is enlivened by numerous steamers ascending and descending the river.

The first point of special interest, above the city, is the mouth of the Missouri; which the party did not wait for upon the upper deck, but went down to the after-guards, and there took their seats to wait until it was passed; and then Alton; and then, just before the gathering twilight, the captain of the boat pointed out, by special request, the locality of the famed "Piasa rock" and cave, in the cliffs that line the river above Alton. Here tradition has preserved the record of one of those surviving monsters of an earlier age, some of which seem to have existed until man came upon the stage; and a cave filled with bones was shown by the Indians, and a rude painting on the tall cliffs marked the spot embalmed in tradition as the scene of an heroic, self-sacrificing deed and a great deliverance. As runs the tradition:

Many hundred (or thousand) moons before the white men came, a monster bird, called by them the Piasa,* of fearful ferocity, size and power, had his haunts in these cliffs, and devoured his prey in the cave near the creek, which to this day bears the name of Piasa. The monster was far more terrible than any of which tradition gives any account, and destroyed great numbers of Indians, as well as deer, buffalo, etc., which he carried to the cave, and there devoured. All attempts to destroy him failed, until finally a young brave, in a lofty spirit of patriotism, proposed a plan, and offered himself as a victim to secure its success.

Accordingly, he was placed in an exposed position near the cave, where the monster would see and swoop down upon him, while near by lay concealed in ambush a chosen band of warriors. The monster returned from a distant flight across the great rivers, and seeing the Indian perched upon a rock near his den, swooped down in fury to destroy him. Like the thunder was the sound of his wings, and like the lightning the fierce flashes from his eyes. But just before the mighty talons grasped the young brave, the Great Spirit interposed an invisible shield over him, and a shower of arrows, from the concealed warriors, pierced the Piasa so that he rolled upon the earth and died, while the hero escaped unharmed; and, in commemoration of this great event, the tribe, with solemn

---

* Piasa, in the language of this tribe, signified Devil Bird.

ceremonies, executed the rude painting upon the face of the cliff, fronting the great Father of Waters.

All listened with intense interest to this interesting relic of the shadowy history of the early ages of this continent, that should as much be preserved in our literature as those of ancient Greece or Rome, or the story of St. George and the dragon, but which will soon have passed into oblivion, unless rescued by some true lover of the shadowy and romantic legends of the past, and of real history and science. For the evidence that much of this tradition is veritable truth, is remarkable, in the bones in the cave, (in enormous quantities within the memory of white men) the painting on the rock, and in geology and natural science.*

It was now dark, and the party withdrew to the cabin to listen to some music from Isabella, her cousin and others, for there was a large company on board from Cincinnati, Louisville, Pittsburg, St. Louis and the south. This entertainment over, and another hour spent in social intercourse, and most of the company retired. But Isabella sat musing in her room upon the heroic chief of the primitive age; and, drawing a parallel in her mind, between him and her absent lover; and then she shuddered at that awful peril of a fiery death; and then her heart glowed with joy and gratitude

"That Heaven had sent her such a man;"

and so, with a full heart and soul, she went to her silent devotions, and then to bed, but not to sleep, until hours had passed.

---

* NOTE.—See Dana's "Text-Book of Geology," pages 172, 182, 183, 201, 230, 231, 239, 241. The early settlers of Alton, Ill., well recollect this famed "Piasa" rock, with the traces of an ancient, rude painting representing the monster, as also the cave in which were quantities of bones of animals, said by the Indians to have been carried there by him. Why our antiquarians and men of science have given such interesting facts so little attention is indeed singular.

CHAPTER XXXII.

ON board the "Northern Belle," politics was again the absorbing topic of discussion, and, as on the other boat, all shades of opinion were represented. Barrona and Doctor Ross took an active part in these discussions, and their views were not generally well received by those on board who talked politics the most; but an appeal to the *voters* on board resulted much the same as on the New Orleans boat, only that being a stranger to the captain the same friendly influence from that quarter was not exercised, and the majority was not so overwhelming, though still large. One gentleman from Cincinnati seemed especially impressed with the importance of a National Constitutional Convention, and of the necessity for abating the wild rush of fanaticism, sectionalism and partisanship; and, on the morning after the discussion was had, and vote taken, he handed to Doctor Ross a paper he had prepared, and which read as follows:

"1776 AND 1860.

"The men of the Revolution were not confident, self-sufficient men; they were men who, while they learned from the wisdom of the past, were practical in the present, and far-sighted in the future. Governed by principle and firm convictions of duty, they seldom yielded to the syren of expediency. Constant and firm of purpose, they possessed none of that stupid obstinacy which, once embarked in a certain course, adheres to it, right or wrong. Washington possessed these high qualities in the most eminent degree. Forming his opinions from established facts, constantly and reverently asking divine aid and guidance, and viewing things as they are; firm in his integrity, constant as the stars, he governed his life by a few simple rules that were in harmony with his character and position, and with the principles of christianity, and true manhood and patriotism. His path was the path of duty and of honor, not the wild comet, flying through the wide realms of space, carrying dismay and terror, but the planet, careering steadily onward in its orbit, governed by fixed laws, and swerved not from truth and right by any wild impulses of ambition or erratic instincts of passion or of fancy. Far different is it now with the great majority of the public men. They do not enquire, ' Is this course *right?* will it promote the best interests of the country?' but, ' Will it win?' Washington's noble rule that 'to men on earth it belongs to deserve success, not to secure it,' has been exactly reversed, and the modern theorist, philosopher, or demagogue, as the case may be, shouts, ' *To secure success is a duty!*' and priests and people say, Amen. The flood-gates are then open for violence and fraud. Hypocrisy robs sincerity of her garments; vice snatches the sword of virtue, and stalks through the land; justice no longer wields power; her seat is usurped by policy, and passion, attended by a crowd of time-servers, fills up all the channels of public opinion. Meantime, our politicians, instead of seeking faithfully the true path of rectitude, and conscientious performance of duty, are diligently watching the horizon to see from which quarter the wind of popular favor will blow, intending to trim their sails accordingly; while 'public opinion,' in turn, is, perhaps, influenced by a few well-prepared, lawyer-like speeches, or newspaper articles, or lying ' statistics.' A vitiated or corrupt press can work untold evil, (until known to be such) and fully verifies the old adage that 'a lie will go a thousand leagues while truth is putting on his boots.' We hope great things from the press for good; but we must not forget that it has also a fearful power for evil, and when steam was applied to the art of printing, error stood ready to use it first. And so it has been. Bold pretenders are everywhere; the trade of the reformer will now be good. The profession of philanthropy, philosophy and humanity will now be profitable. Religion, betrayed and perverted by corrupt priests, will be taken from the service of Christ and harnessed to the car of politics. Hypocrisy will thrive; rant, cant and fustian, will pass current as pure gold. There will be a fearful plowing and harrowing, nominally in the interest of virtue, religion and truth; but when the crop has ripened, the fruit will betray the vile seed; for God's laws of reproduction are immutable, in the moral, as in the physical world, and cannot be cheated."

The little group before whom this short paper was read sat silent for some moments after its reading was concluded. At length a gentleman from Indiana spoke:

"Evidently, the writer of this has not a good opinion of his own times, and, it seems to me, is somewhat ruthless in running the plow-share through everything that most men revere."

"I yield to none," said the Cincinnati man, "in reverence for the good and true, but I think it right, in view of the fallibility and error in all human affairs, to apply to the test from Holy Writ: 'By their fruits ye shall know them;' and in this way I conclude that much is error that passes current for truth, and error of the most infernal kind."

"Yes," said the other, "but, in trying to uproot error,

you will tear up truth too; you should remember the parable of our Savior, and leave the tares with the wheat until harvest, lest, in seeking to get rid of one, you destroy both."

"The beauty, force and truth of that illustration we admire," replied Cincinnati, "but must bear in mind that it relates to future judgment, under God's government, and not to the present duty of opposing error; moreover, in its application, we can remember that all fields of grain are not wheat-fields, nor are all situations of error alike. In our *corn-fields*, we plow up the weeds and leave the corn, and so secure a good crop, which otherwise the weeds would destroy or render unfruitful; the corn being planted in exact rows and hills, renders this possible, which would not be with wheat sown broadcast. So in our most highly-favored age and country; with the benign light of christianity, and the straight rows of well-established society, constitutional government and science, we should be able, by peaceful beneficent constitutional means, to cultivate truth, and subdue errors and hypocrisies in public affairs; and so now we should resort to the peaceful means of a constitutional convention, and so cultivate the field, rather than endorse 'Helper's Crisis,' and so risk the tearing up and destruction of the whole crop, truth and error included; for the danger is that this violence and perversion of truth may bring on civil war, and, though the *forms* of our grand government might last for a time in spite of so rude a shock, yet it would certainly jeopardize its *vital principle*, which is the mutual interest and good will of the people, which should be maintained by kind and honorable dealing between the different sections."

"I believe you are right," replied the gentleman from Indiana; "but I think you over-estimate the danger."

Here the bell rang for dinner, and the discussion ended.

CHAPTER XXXIII.

WE have said that the company on board this northern-bound steamer was large It was also brilliant and fashionable.

Isabella, as we have said, was no devotee of fashion; but yet she was not at all dazzled, blinded or confused by the style and tone of fashionable society, but quite at her ease and self-possessed, as if among her own chosen friends at home. And she soon had many friends and some admirers.

On board the boat was a certain handsome and fashionable gentleman from New York, of very great wealth, and quite a lion in society. This gentleman was acquainted with some St. Louis and Louisiana people, with whom Barrona was acquainted, and so was introduced to him, and by him to his family and to Isabella, to whom he at once showed great attention, which she received as a matter of courtesy, and showed a gentle courtesy in return. But Mr. Bell, for that was the gentleman's name, meant more than courtesy, and could not understand Isabella's manner on any other hypothesis than that which he was accustomed to find current, that is, that the ladies were ready and willing to be captivated by his fine person, talents, polished manners and immense fortune; and Isabella was so ingenuous and true that she could not think of anything of this kind. But he was too discerning not to soon see through his error; yet this only fascinated him the more. Great, then, was his chagrin when he learned that this "Pearl of the South," as he called her, had given her heart, and was soon to give her hand, to a northern raftsman, whose whole fortune did not amount to his income for a single month. His resolution was at once taken: he determined to win this southern girl if money could do it; and he cultivated a close acquaintance at once with Barrona. But Barrona was too well acquainted with the world and with men not to see through his design, and, yielding to his friendly advances, was soon on terms that he could with propriety speak of his daughter's engagement and of Sydenham, in terms that closed the door forever against further advances in that direction.

Isabella, in a state of joyous anticipation and impatience, in the expectation of soon meeting again her lover, did not dream of the conquest she had made, and treated Mr. Bell, as she did all her other acquaintances, with genial courtesy and freedom. In this frame of mind, on the second evening after leaving St. Louis, she accepted Mr. Bell's invitation to walk on the hurricane deck. Glowing with the thought of seeing him who filled her thoughts on the next morning, she was gay and joyous, and talked with vivacity and interest. With consummate tact, and using all his great conversational powers, he turned the conversation upon everything splendid, rich and grand, in America and Europe, upon all the delights and splendors of Paris, the grandeur of Rome, the beautiful land of Spain, (her mother's birthplace) the classic shores of the Mediterranean, the grandeur of courts, the treasures of art and genius, and all, in short, that unbounded and well-used wealth could command. To all this Isabella listened with the greatest interest and pleasure, and she did not conceal her admiration in the slightest, either of the subjects or of the splendid conversational powers of this elegant and handsome stranger; for she really was greatly interested and delighted, just as she would have been in hearing a fine actor declaim from the stage. He then went on to describe how he had longed to fit out a splendid steam yacht, whose cabins should be gorgeous as a fairy tale, whose strength and speed set danger at defiance, and in it to sail for England, then France, then Spain, thence to Italy, thence to Greece, Egypt, Constantinople and the shores of Palestine.

"Ah," said Isabella, "that would be most delightful and grand, indeed, to see all that is so interesting, rare and wonderful on the earth; and I almost envy you the trip."

"You need not," said Bell, "for I would be too miserable to be envied, unless I have a companion in it."

"Indeed," said Isabella, "but you will have a companion, of course."

"That, Miss Barrona, I cannot tell, for it depends upon another."

"If that is all," said Isabella, innocently, "you should not be disappointed, for no one would refuse so delightful a trip."

"I rejoice to hear you say so," said Bell, in a deep, low, earnest tone, "for you are the one upon whom it depends."

"How, Mr. Bell, what do you mean?" said Isabella, starting abruptly.

"Pardon me, Miss Barrona," said he, in a low tone, "you may think I am too bold, and presume too much for so brief an acquaintance as we have had, but I feel that I must say to you, *to-night*, what I should have deferred until you had known me longer; but I offer you to-night my hand, my heart and my fortune."

"Mr. Bell," said Isabella, starting, "you surprise me.

Did not my father tell you that I loved another, and that my hand was pledged *to him?*"

Mr. Bell stammered and hesitated; for there was that in the simple, direct question of the lady before him, and its calm tone, that turned him back as he had never before been turned back in the pursuit of any object. But she waited for his answer, and he had to give it, and to admit that he had been told, but he hoped he might yet win her; he plead his love, and again painted the splendor, boundless wealth and pleasure, that should be hers, and he her slave, and she a queen, instead of the wife of an obscure raftsman.

Isabella heard him quietly to the end, so quietly that he thought he might win her; and when he concluded he took her hand. Then she started back; and, like the lightning's flash, her glance pierced him, and her words, like cold steel, cut down at a stroke the arrogant presumption of immense wealth and high position—fostered and nourished for a whole lifetime.

"Sir, I am not for sale. My love I have given to another: and if you were the monarch of those countries you propose visiting in such splendor, I would not be tempted, in the slightest, to give you my hand and be your queen when I loved Walter Sydeham, and we were soon to be united. And oh! 'He is but a poor, obscure raftsman!' Ah, yes, but he holds a patent of nobility from the Most High, Himself, and this all your wealth will not buy. So, Isabella Barrona goes to the arms of a richer man than you, and a nobler, and a braver; for *you* come as a tempter and a thief. Away from me! let me go to my mother."

And so, with a wave of her hand, and a proud step, she descended alone to her mother's room; and there, with sobs and tears, told her all of her temptation.

CHAPTER XXXIV.

AS nature is never more lovely than after a summer shower, when the lightning of heaven has purified the air, and the falling rain has refreshed the earth, so, never did Isabella appear more beautiful, and almost sublime in its expression, than on the following morning. As the boat neared Rock Island, she went on deck with her father, and endeavored to see if Sydenham was in the crowd of people who thronged the steamboat-landing. At length she saw him, standing a little back from the crowd, and watching the boat intently. She waved her handkerchief, and he instantly saw and answered the signal. As the boat landed, she descended to her mother's room, and there received him with as much joy as though they had been separated for months, or years, instead of only four days.

As for Sydenham, he had almost reasoned himself into the belief that, in the caprice of fortune, it could not be *possible* that such immense happiness should be his longer than a few days, and that some accident or disaster must, in the nature of things, occur, to prevent a happy meeting, and interrupt his marriage; and when he told Isabella this, she smiled archly, and leaned her head upon his shoulder, while her mother related what had happened. To this Sydenham listened with a swelling heart, but with some pangs, at the thought of his own poverty, and at her sacrifice for him. And he told her this, and then how it happened that he had been prompted, other than by his love and hope, to dare to ask her hand.

Isabella listened to the story of Grey Eagle's death with wonder; and when Sydenham narrated the prophetic vision of the dying chief, her emotions were quite beyond control; and Barrona, his wife and Mrs. Johnson, (who was present with Doctor Ross, by Sydenham's request) were all deeply affected, and saw, with awe and wonder, the mysterious links in this chain of strange and unwonted events, as though the spiritual and infinite had joined in this mysterious web of destiny, in saving the lives of those on board the Comet, and giving this pair to each other.

"Now," said Isabella, fondly, "I know I did well in resisting this tempter, this handsome adorer, with his five millions, and taking this raftsman; and if ever I repent, you may produce this book of destiny; and if ever you repent, I will remind you of this five millions, &c.; and so we are even," she said, smiling, and gently pressing her hands upon his head; "and now go and bring Grey Eagle's rifle and hunting gear."

These were examined with deep interest by Barrona and the ladies, who all expressed a wish to visit the mysterious cave, and the secluded romantic valley, with its dells and waterfalls; and it was arranged that a small dwelling should be erected on the ground occupied by Grey Eagle's lodge, so that the party could visit it after the marriage at St. Paul. And now the polite steward knocked at the door and announced dinner.

Mr. Bell, it now appeared, had left the boat at Rock Island, and taken the cars for Chicago; and so the party were relieved from any embarrassment; and, in the presence of so large and gay a company, he was soon forgotten.

In the evening, on the upper deck, Isabella related to

her lover the legend of the Piasa, and he pointed out to her various objects of interest along the shores, with which, from Rock Island to St. Paul, he was familiar. Mrs. Johnson and Doctor Ross sat near, and she seemed greatly interested in the story of Grey Eagle, and all relating to the cave, the lofty dome above it, &c., all which the Doctor promised to show her, and to write out for her the entire story, and the death-song of Grey Eagle; she promising to repay him by writing an account for him of the escape from the Comet, and a copy of a short poem she had composed upon that event.

"These manuscripts," said the Doctor, "we can place in our library."

"Yes," said the lady, "they will form quite an addition to our libraries; and I will do my best to make mine interesting."

"I only hope," said the Doctor, "I may succeed in making mine interesting, and worthy to be read by you, dear madam."

"How," said the lady, "could it be otherwise than worthy and interesting, when written by my noble friend, Doctor Ross, who snatched me from the very jaws of death itself."

Sydenham and Isabella rose and walked forward. They were then alone. The evening was balmy and glorious; the moon was rising over the bluffs; love was in the air; the sweet contagion had seized upon both;—who could doubt the result? In less than fifteen minutes the stately lady had accepted the hand of the gallant Doctor, and before they left the deck he had gained her consent to keep her niece company, and celebrate their nuptials at St. Paul, instead of awaiting their return to Louisiana.

"For," said the lovely lady, "we can sometimes afford

to do what we know to be right, proper and conducive to the happiness of our friends and ourselves, even if it is not in strict accord with the conventionalities of fashion. My friends in Louisiana will be surprised, doubtless, but I think they will approve, as I know my brother and his family will, and Isabella will be delighted; and will you, my dear friend, *truly* approve?" said the lady, smiling inquiringly.

"No," said the Doctor, "I will not approve; that word is too tame, unless we multiply it a thousand-fold, or so; say I ten thousand times approve it, and it will do."

CHAPTER XXXV.

OUR tale is now drawing to a close, as it is expected a love story should, on the marriage of the parties, it being usually expected that *then* romance ends, and practical life begins. We propose to conform to the rules, although the adventures of the characters of our story, during the five years succeeding, would be sufficiently varied and thrilling to form the subject matter for several books.

Within two weeks after the arrival of the party at St. Paul, the marriage of Isabella and Sydenham took place; and, at the same time, that of Dr. Ross and Mrs. Johnson. Shortly after this, the two newly married pairs took the packet for Grey Eagle Valley, where a neat and cosy dwelling, built of pine lumber, was finished and ready for them; and here, in this "lodge in the wilderness," in the midst of these cool, sylvan shades, they spent the remainder of the summer, Barrona and the rest of the party remaining at St. Paul, or the places of interest in the vicinity, most of the time. About the beginning of September, all were collected at the lodge, and, on the second morning after, climbed to the summit of the dome-like peak of the bluff, over the cave, and looked out upon the grand panorama below and around them. The whole party were delighted with the beauty of the prospect, but Isabella seemed sad, and, after a long silence, said:

"My father, you have often told me our country is one, and that the different States are all united in one body, the United States."

"My child," said Barrona, tenderly kissing her on the forehead, "you are quite right; they are, or should be, united; and loyalty to one, means loyalty to all; and patriotism means love of country therefore, the whole country. But why do you ask?"

"Because," said Isabella, "I wish we could all live here, in Minnesota, where there is no malaria, nor yellow fever, and health and vigor is the rule. You know, father, I love my home in the south, and our colored people could not bear to have me leave them, but I have often heard you speak with regret of the deadly diseases we are subject to there, and wish it were otherwise, so that part of the summer and fall would not be so dreaded. Do you know, Walter does not wish to go to Louisiana to live, but wants to stay here, and wants you should all come here and settle, and make a new home in the north?"

"I have thought of all this," said Barrona, sadly, "and I believe it best that you and he should do so; and it is right; but I cannot feel that it is right for *me*, at least not now. For, although I might wish to do so, I could not; nor, however much I might like the north, and hold to a sentiment of broad nationality that knows neither north nor south, I could not feel it right to make such a change on the eve of great troubles, which will probably be greater for the south than the north. I *hope* there will be none of either; yet, in the crisis, if there is to be one, my place is at home, But you, my daughter, and Walter, are differently situated. *This is his home*, therefore it is yours; on the same great river, but further north. It is hard to part with you, my dear child; but your mother left her native land when she married me, because my home was in America; and it was best and right for her to do so. She crossed the seas, but you only go a few hundred miles up the great river, on whose banks you were born. So do not weep, my child, for you will visit us, after a time, and we will visit you; and perhaps Walter may move to Louisiana, in time, or I to Minnesota, or both to some intermediate parallel of latitude, well fitted for the health and well-being of both ourselves and our posterity; for I bear in mind that portion of Grey Eagle's prophesy, as well as that we see fulfilled, and hope," he said, turning to Walter, who stood beside his wife, (her hand in his) " that a blessing may indeed rest upon your house, to the remotest generations. You, my children," he continued, " have been most richly blessed in each other's love, and in all other things. So let us, here and now, worship our Creator, and return thanks for his favor, and invoke its continuance."

And there, on the summit of the lofty bluff, under the shade of an oak, all kneeled in prayer; and then Isabella broke forth in song, in which nearly all joined. And so their vine was planted, their household altar established, and love's victory was completely won.

But while thus, this serene light of virtue, peace and love, spread over this secluded dell, the dark cloud on the political horizon had grown larger and larger; and larger yet it grew. And the time will surely come when it will be asked why the safe constitutional haven was not sought by any; why sectionalism and partisanship still held sway, and why WAR finally swept over the land. We think we have already answered these questions; but they are with the past, and with the past let them remain. When it shall be asked whether the government of Washington and his compeers was so faulty that it could stand no longer without a war to maintain it, then may history unravel some webs of error, and weave anew from the plain, incontrovertible facts that are found upon the very surface, and accord with the theory and genius of the constitution and government, a record that shall stand for all time; a warning against violent resorts, rebellion, and warfare against the good and true, whether that rebellion be open or covert, and, an incentive to—"THAT MAGNANIMOUS PUBLIC POLICY WHICH BRINGS THE SOLID REWARDS OF PROSPERITY AND HAPPINESS," and accords with true religion. The Duke of Wellington said that "war, after all, was no remedy," and we may well pause and inquire if this expression of the Iron Duke we have not proved true? Even now we feel the want, daily and hourly growing greater and greater, of a re-adjustment of the lost balance; of the giving back to the people of the States; the power that is theirs; of the refreshing of the principles of the constitution, and, *instead of contending for laws in regard to national finances, national debt, &c.*, simply ENGRAFT PERMANENTLY UPON THE CONSTITUTION AN EQUITABLE POLICY RELATING THERETO, thus REMOVING *these vexed questions, and endless sources of* CORRUPTION, *forever from the halls of* CONGRESS *and from the arena of party strife;* removing, also, the causes of much *jealousy, and strife of classes*, with *all its evils and dangers.*

Happy will be the day when the people of America, forgetting or forgiving the past, shall meet in a National Constitutional Convention; and great are the abuses it will reform; and great the dangers and troubles, and enormous and augmenting the evils that demand it. Let it be held speedily; and happy will be the memory of it for the ages to come, and glorious the immediate results.

THE END.

APPENDIX.

"I like to see gentlemen as prodigal of their own blood as they are of the blood of other people."—*Gen. Shields.*

"Are the christian nations patterns of charity and forbearance? On the contrary, their principal business is to destroy each other. More than five millions of christians are trained, educated and drilled, to murder their fellow-christians. Every nation is groaning under a vast debt incurred in carrying on war against other christians, or defending themselves from christian assault. The world is covered with forts to protect christians from christians; and every sea is covered with iron monsters ready to blow christian brains into eternal froth. Millions upon Millions are annually expended in the effort to construct still more deadly and terrible engines of death. Industry is crippled, honest toil is robbed, and even beggary is taxed to defray the expenses of christian warfare, There must be some other way to reform this world."—*Ingersol.*

Since this little book was written, the tragic and ghastly farce of "Military Glory" has been performed upon a mighty scale in Europe, with an afterpiece by Thiers and the Communists, yet more deplorable. Many wars seem necessary evils, and can point to results that are beneficent. But can these? Has any good result been won? If so, could it not have been better won by a convention? And the working men of Paris, that class that stood forward so prominently in the Great Revolution of 1790, afterwards the right hand of France, when France stood as a giant, confronting and defeating embattled Europe, ranged under the banners of absolutism; a class that, whatever its faults, (which are not so great as its sufferings) has not been equaled, since the days of the Democracy of Ancient Greece and Rome, for heroic, self-sacrificing patriotism and valor—these men are driven into a desperate conflict, deformed by the mad frenzy of despair, and at its close are butchered and in many cases their wives with them. And the directors of what is called the Versailles government, and who refused compromise with their countrymen, and rejected their oft-repeated overtures, and that of the Masonic bodies, were men who had not risked one drop of their blood, or one hair of their heads in defence of their country when it was being ground under the heel of a foreign invader. They succeeded, through havoc and ruin; but would not a magnanimous policy have better secured the solid results of public prosperity and happiness? But despotism, in all its varied forms, is cowardly, though clothed in triple mail—"prodigal of the blood of other people," cruel, and *cannot* be magnanimous.

The Thiers government has now formed a mutual Admiration Society, and appear to enjoy themselves; but does it repose upon the good will of the people? Has the volcano been extinguished by the blood that was poured into it? The Paris correspondent of the London *Times* writes that the Workingmen's International Association in Europe, for the promotion of a Universal Republic, numbers two millions and a half of men. Some of these men's views may be utopian, impracticable and wrong, but they all clearly discern the old stupidities of military ambition, vast standing armies, useless wars, and their interminable burthens, and recognize many cardinal principles of common sense, humanity and pure christianity. Bismarck's eye is upon them, and he cannot brook that one of them should hold an humble position for the United States government on Prussian soil. So the policy in Europe is, in the future as in the past, to be *suppression*, not COMPROMISE. The world is said to be exceedingly wise at this present day—very enlightened, polished and humane, but it has a curious way of showing it.

Some such a convocation as that held in England, at Runnymede, some centuries ago, when school-masters were very scarce, and newspapers scarcer, would do even for these wise times; but if held, it would not promote the cause of absolutism, or demagoguism, or hypocricy, or fanaticism, or public plunder. Have these things suppressed true manhood, and rendered useless the teachings of history and experience, and the application of plain truth divested of theory impossible? If we lift the gorgeous curtain of this European military glory, we see behind it the old features of despotism, and the gaunt forms of poverty and woe; and in our own land, if we lift the curtain of Reconstruction, on which is painted a caricature of universal suffrage, we see behind it the corrupt adventurers making off with the spoils—say to the extent of thirty-five millions from one plundered, impoverished and ruined State. Well may the atheist scoff and point the finger of scorn at what he calls christian government. Well may men despair, when violence and corruption, fanaticism and plunder join hands and are so often successful. It is related of Bruce, that when defeated and overborne, he took refuge in a cave, and was upon the brink of despair, he gained new courage from watching an ant endeavoring to carry a grain of wheat up a steep ascent, and after many failures, succeeding; and so his royal heart renewed its hope. Truth is now a poor fugitive, and her place has been usurped. Even the voice of Lincoln denounces from his grave the things that have been done. And there is no hope in any political party, anxious only for office and power; but in the great castle of God's eternal truth, whose gates are not kept by any priest, is the record of our land. And there, in the chamber (or vault) of the American Constitution, is the provision for the convocation of the States.

CHICAGO, July 27, 1871.

ERRATA.

The publishers would apologise to the public for the errors that have crept into this work, as is generally the case in *first* editions, the most palpable of which are pointed out below:

PAGE 99. "We *expend* too fast in everything," should be *expand*.
PAGE 135. "The *tide waters* of the Missouri," should read: The *turbid tide*.
PAGE 135. "Earthy *water*" should read: Earthy *matter*.
PAGE 137. "Mississippi river; towns," should be Mississippi river towns;
PAGE 144. "South-*western* extremity of Iowa," should read: South-*eastern*.
PAGE 157. For "*Sloshed*" read *slashed*.
PAGE 194. For "*Radical* element dominated," read: *Conservative* element dominated.

www.ingramcontent.com/pod-product-compliance
Lightning Source LLC
Chambersburg PA
CBHW021820230426

43669CB00008B/815